## Praise for *Sufism for Western Seekers*

- Years of study and walking in two modern day mystical schools, operating in the West, have given the author Dr. Stewart Bitkoff valuable guidance to pass on his contribution to the present and next generations of seekers. This book *Sufism for Western Seekers* is a testimony to that transmission. The language is easy, written by the ink of one's direct experience with a self-effacing Spiritual Teacher. By God's permission, the Book will be beneficial for all seekers, whether from East or West, whether following the Sufi Path or not. Truth manifests by Itself and sincere seekers shall recognize this in these pages.

  Sadiq M. Alam, Dhaka, Bangladesh
  Author and Editor of the site, Technology of the Heart (www.mysticsaint.info)

- In this book, Dr. Bitkoff uses stories and examples from modern America to show how the ancient wisdom of Sufism can be used to enrich contemporary life. Clear, accessible and inspiring for anyone seeking guidance on a spiritual journey. A treasure!

  Sheikha Halima Haymaker, Santa Rosa, CA

- In poetry, prose, allegory and narrative Dr. Bitkoff peels back the inner world of Sufism for the western reader. He generously shares stories from his past, steps along his journey, mistakes made and roads not taken. He makes it possible for us to absorb the gentle message of the oneness of creation and our place within it. There is traditional learning within these pages as well as inner meaning that seeps into us from between the words. Like seeds which ripen in its own time, these buds of knowledge can take root within us and, if the time and place are right, blossom into the type of understanding that will stay with you long after you have finished reading this book.

  Michael Greenstein, MS, Dobbs Ferry, NY

- Dr. Bitkoff has created a unique book that not only educates and motivates, but is down right fun to read. The book mirrors his personal and spiritual growth with details from his life. In the fashion of Master-Student we are invited to share his wisdom and learn. He has given us a road map to reach God (The Light). He believes Sufism predates all religions and is innately within all of us. In the Buddhist fashion, we are advised to make up our own minds about everything. However, the stories and parables he shares have led this reader to agree with his thoughts. The book is well worth reading and is fun.

Stephen Taus, MD, Ranchos Palos Verdes, CA

# SUFISM FOR WESTERN SEEKERS

# Sufism
# for
# Western Seekers

*Path of the Spiritual Traveler
in Everyday Life*

Dr. Stewart Bitkoff

Abandoned Ladder

Printed in the United States of America

ISBN-13: 978-0615562803 (Abandoned Ladder)
ISBN-10: 0615562809

10 9 8 7 6 5 4 3 2 1

## A Sam Story[1]

Once there was a spiritual traveler who like other men worked, had a family, and helped care for his home and community. Additionally, this man was blessed with the capacity to explain some of the eternal truths in beautiful, written language. However, something was lacking in his writing and it had limited use.

As the years wore on and this man struggled with adversity and sickness, something happened. Gradually, a softness and tenderness appeared in his writings. This was the missing ingredient, and as it was added, thousands were able to derive benefit.

*         *

---

[1]As per his wishes, to shield the teacher's identity, Sam is a pseudonym used throughout this manuscript.

# Contents

# Acknowledgements

From a spiritual perspective, one of the central aspects to life concerns learning from daily experience and realizing just about any set of circumstances can teach you something. Over the last 2 years, working on this manuscript has taught me about myself, other people, and the publishing process. My hope is that this combination of factors resulted in a richer, more informative read for the spiritual traveler who picks up this book.

My thanks to Jennine Cabrera, Noah Greenstein and Dr. Andrew Mezurecky for help developing this manuscript and getting the material ready for the publisher.

Additionally, thanks to Sam, Zach, Eddie, Paul, Ben, Steve and other spiritual travelers who were there in the beginning.

Working on this material, again has reminded me of the wonderful heritage of Sufi learning and great teachers who came before and help provide direction far into the future. These are the hidden friends of humanity, helping us daily to reach higher,

Finally, thanks to my family/friends: Lea, Melody, Holly, Greg, Abby, Emily, Caity, Kelly, Lou, Rose, Mollie, Bruce, Jeff, Brenda, Mike and Marty; all who have shown me that love truly 'rules the planets.' Also, all life's going and doing means very little unless there are people you love and care about to share joy, learning and experience.

# Introduction

Many people, at some point in their lives, think, "I should write a book about my favorite subject; I have so much to say." Often, I've come across others who even have had a first shot at their manuscript. Usually, it's buried in their closets, of course, far from seeing the light of day; but nevertheless, most of us have "the next bestseller" in our hearts.

My experience has been somewhat different. I've been writing for a long time, and I actually self-published several books. I've kept at it for most of my adult life. A few years back, I revisited one of these self-published books, did some editing, added a marketing plan and some publicity, and embarked on a journey that culminated in the publication of A Commuter's Guide to Enlightenment* in March 2008. "A dream come true," you may think to yourself. But life is funny that way, isn't it? You really do have to be careful what you wish for.

The experience of being published was at once exciting and disappointing. I had hoped to reach many, yet sales were not that strong. Although disappointed, I was not discouraged. My desire to reach my fellow spiritual travelers is still as vibrant as ever. For a follow-up, I realized that I had to take a different approach.

This present writing, as the Sufis would say, came about through 'a confluence of essences.' While offering a first hand account of learning in two modern Sufi schools, it also presents how this learning is useful in daily life. Over a period of months, I searched for a topic that I felt strongly about and could draw interest from today's western spiritual traveler. I thought a book on mysticism, as taught in a western Sufi school, might be a good place to begin. Although immersed in this topic, I have never considered myself an expert or thought about writing specifically on this subject. I decided to embark upon this project in the hope that I might add a new voice to the mix.

Somehow all of this came together, and what I present to you here are a series of reflections and discussions about some of the basic questions facing all spiritual travelers along the Path. Whether we realize it or not, all of our lives are spent on a spiritual journey; indeed, every one of us is a spiritual traveler. When faced with crises of spirit in our lives, we often erroneously think that we must retreat or isolate ourselves from the "day-to-day" in order to follow our spiritual nature. In fact, the opposite is often true, there is much learning and enlightenment to be found in what would otherwise be considered mundane or ordinary.

Enlightenment can be achieved in daily life, doing just about anything; and both sets of consciousness, the everyday and the spiritual, operate simultaneously. Like an onion, our levels of consciousness and awareness are multiple; in time, the spiritual traveler learns to operate multiple levels, to help self and others reach toward complete, balanced living. Traditionally, this is the ancient, natural way of spiritual development. The course of study is individual, unique to the specific person, and the outcome of this teaching is a spiritual traveler who is able to use his higher capacity in everyday life to help self and others.

It is my hope that in reading and learning about these spiritual experiences, you will be inspired to strive for your own higher purpose everyday along the Path.

> I searched for God and found only myself.
> I searched for myself and found only God.
>
> Sufi Proverb

# What is Sufism?

**Traveler:** *When friends ask me what I study, and I try to explain, I find it hard to put into words, what is Sufism? Help me understand so I can give a clearer explanation.*

**Master:** *One of the great teachers offered, 'long before there was a name (Sufism) there was a reality. Now there is a name without a reality.' What is meant by this is that there has always been a way to connect with and experience ultimate Truth; this spiritual path of learning existed long before travelers, in the late 1800's, gave this way of learning its present name-Sufism. At the time, local ascetics wore a distinctive woolen (soof) robe and became known for this. Now this name, or spiritual form, for many followers exists without a corresponding inner reality. Often today, what you see in the world represented as Sufism is an empty shell of its former self.*

*This ancient Path of spiritual development is based upon connection with and experience of the Divine. This connection occurs in daily life doing a variety of seemingly ordinary activities. It involves study with a teacher and the awakening, through direct contact with Truth, of latent spiritual capacity; this is done so the traveler can help others. This Truth or universal essence, the spiritual traveler seeks and experiences, is the underlying energy or fabric of created forms.*

*This Path existed long before there were religions; this way of learning is at the heart of the great religions; it is the underlying spiritual energy that gives everything in the universe its form and substance. Inside each of us is an aspect of this wondrous element. Through preparation, practice developing our inner spiritual awareness, and Grace we unite with and serve Ultimate Reality every day.*

*My teacher called this Path - the Superhighway to God. For those who wish to connect with Truth and use their inner spiritual capacity to help others; this form of learning is available in every town and city.*

*Sufism is not something talked about or described in written words; it is a universal essence that is experienced and known through inner spiritual contact. Much like love; no matter how many words you use- the description is not the same as the actual experience. And like love which ebbs and flows, Sufism changes to fit the learner, time and place.*

**Traveler:** *This helps a little. Sufism is difficult to put into words because it is a spiritual experience and changes with each person. Yet, I have been in love and know there are different forms of love with many peaks and valleys that are impossible to describe; and no matter how pretty a poem or love song, it is not the experience itself.*

**Master:** *Remember, everyone is a spiritual traveler and in their long journey through this universe, experiences many wondrous things. Countless experiences go beyond words and cannot be written down—changing with each moment and person. This dimension is one of the elements that make life so complex and beautiful. If this is too difficult for those who ask about us to grasp, ask them to define love or even life itself. As they ponder all the possibilities then they will begin to understand.*

\*      \*

# — 1 —

# My Religious Training

I was raised Jewish in New York City; on my father's side of the family we were descendants of Rabbis and according to our grandparents, my great grandfather was a renowned philanthropist, teacher and Rabbi in the old country before their lands were seized by the Czar.

To me, my early religious training was very confusing; very little of it made any sense and much of it was in Hebrew, a language I couldn't understand. There were ancient customs I couldn't connect with; and the old stories of the prophets held no real meaning for me. Conversely, both of my grandfathers found great joy and comfort being part of their congregations; and I loved and respected them very much.

Also, both my parents had their own way of adapting. For the most part, my father was too busy trying to make a living to care much about all of this; although he tried to follow the old traditions as best he could. While my mother used to laugh at some of the 'old black costumes or traditional dress' that conservative Jewish people wore, particularly, in the summer 90 degree heat; she used to say, these clothes were not practical and they were not trying very hard to fit into American life. Further, she loved to watch the Evangelist, Billy Graham on television, and had her own private way of talking with God.

Meanwhile on the streets of Manhattan, I was constantly getting into fights, because I was Jewish. Sometimes, the other Christian kids would hide behind parked cars on the street, just outside the

1

temple exit, and pound us with rocks as we came out from Hebrew school. Whenever possible, I would find one of them and as pay back- kick their butt. At the time, getting even made more sense to me, than, the things I was learning inside the temple walls.

To me, it was all about survival and ignorance. Here, there were a bunch of kids waiting to pound on me for my beliefs, which at the time, I did not believe. Go figure. So in order to survive I had to take the necessary action. Nowadays, sort of what is still going on in the Middle East; only with a more deadly outcome? Religion is being used as a smoke screen for a power play; one group of people being taught they are right and the other is wrong, so, they can feel good about themselves and take something from the other. Perhaps, it was no different back then, as well, in the old neighborhood. Some kids getting their excitement, using religion, to pound on someone else.

I have to say, that much of my life did not really make much sense to me, until my mid and early 20's. I was sort of drifting from one thing to another; trying to do the right thing, but not having anything, inwardly, to hold onto and provide direction. Yet, all about me 'the times were a changing' and were exciting; the 60's and early 70's- all kinds of things were going on and I experimented like others, but could not connect, inwardly, with anything, on a lasting basis.

From a spiritual perspective, the early part of my life was a preparation for my moment of awakening, although I didn't realize it at the time. Certainly, there were people and experiences I felt deeply about. In the quiet moments, when my mind was not filled with people whom I loved or my work and school, this lack of inner peace and direction pushed me onward. Inwardly, I was continually searching for an answer to the question, why are we here? Why is this world so transitory? What is life, which is so full of joy and pain, really about?

For many people, it is the religion of their birth that answers this kind of question; their religion provides an inner foundation and basis from which to build their lives. For me, I had to sip of another cup; not being inwardly satisfied with any religion or philosophy, until I found and experienced the Light.

Inwardly, I was not at ease and the last place I looked for personal comfort was religion; no one had ever told me there was a difference between an outer teaching, or religious form, and the inner experience, or essence, of religious teaching. Inwardly, at their higher levels, all the great religions are One; and this primordial energy which gives them substance and life is holistic, vibrant, Loving and under the right circumstances, could be experienced, individually and collectively.

And all my inward searching; being lost, hurt, lonely and restless was a preparation for that moment of awakening. The cup had been empty, so the Light could fill it and alter the direction of my life. And in order for any life to have real meaning you must feel passionately about something, like the songbird you have to have a song to sing, and I was looking for mine. The 'great emptiness or hunger' was pushing me onward.

Within each person there is an 'empty space' that is waiting to be filled by the 'Light of God;' this emptiness manifests as an unease, a discomforting fear and ache; it is this unease, a friction of sorts that drives people onward, seeking to fill this void with all kinds of things. The world is filled with many stimuli and the traveler, unless awakened, will try to quiet this primordial unease and resulting fear and anxiety by mentally attaching their consciousness and body to just about anything.

Spiritual awakening is like the sunrise of a new day, filling the traveler with hope and joy- transcending time and space in one glorious moment of understanding. It is an explosion of energy that lifts the traveler onto a new path; setting the heart aglow with love, higher knowledge and deep peace. This happened for me through my participation in a modern Sufi school.

\*       \*

— 2 —

# Getting Started

### The Sufi Quest

Man, we say we know, originates from far away; so far, indeed, that in speaking of his origin, such phrases as 'beyond the stars' are frequently employed. Man is estranged from his origins. Some of his feelings (but not all of them) are slight indicators of this ... Man has the opportunity of returning to his origin. He has forgotten this. He is, in fact, 'asleep' to this reality. Sufism is designed as the means to help awaken man to this realization, not just the opinion, of the above statements. Those who awaken are able to return, to start 'the journey' while living the present life in all its fullness. Traditions about monasticism and isolation are reflections of short-term processes of training or development, monstrously misunderstood and grotesquely elaborated to provide refuges for those who want to stay asleep

Mevlevi

This quote by Mevlevi describes what the spiritual traveler sets out to accomplish: Awaken a part of self that has long been asleep; in order to enrich the traveler's life. This process or spiritual path is a very ancient one, predating formal religious teaching and, held

4

among its followers to be the underlying unity, or common mystical experience inherent in all religious forms. I hope to help you become more awakened by sharing the following:

1. *Updated Teaching.* Sufism is a living vibrant element and is constantly evolving and being updated. Its universal energy can lift you up and alter your life. Its learning stretches across a lifetime and changes people, one person at a time. This timeless teaching changes to fit the traveler and the times. Herein, is a presentation of this teaching that was offered to a group of western spiritual travelers; no one had to put on an exotic garb, follow a different religion or leave their work and family to drink of this wondrous element. It was offered within the context of everyday life; in a large city, at work- in a psychiatric hospital, and during lunchtime. Appealing to travelers from all religious backgrounds- it is a 'generic universal mysticism,' that according to tradition, is at the heart of all religious teachings. What was offered was an experience of a timeless, ancient teaching that was updated into modern language using question and answer. Yet beneath this verbal exchange was a palpable spiritual experience of energy, an essence that transcended the moment and connected us to universal consciousness. To the Sufi, this caress is called 'the Beloved's Kiss,' and proves to the traveler there is a reality beyond our daily lives that has always loved us.

2. *Insider View.* Typically, most books on Sufism are written by academics, whose experience is a scholarly one as opposed to an actual spiritual traveler who has been initiated, embraced and has experienced the inner reality. Accordingly, this writing offers a first hand retrospective view of what takes place between the master, who for purposes of confidentiality is called Sam, and an individual traveler, as opposed to what different experts and authorities have studied and "translated." Then, the story follows the traveler to the next school, and offers a practical discussion of the levels of learning encountered, across the years, in daily life.

3. *Nutrient to Life.* According to one of the great teachers, Sufism is a nutrient that enables the traveler to become spiritually developed; it is the missing ingredient and fills the 'great hunger,' which propels us all forward in search of higher meaning and purpose. Throughout this work, there are numerous examples of how this perspective or nutrient can be helpful.

4. *Levels of Awareness.* According to the Sufi, enlightenment can be achieved in ordinary life, doing just about anything; and both sets of consciousness- everyday and spiritual- after a period of preparation, operate simultaneously. This narrative utilizes a conversational device of one aspect of consciousness, everyday awareness, talking to the higher aspect, spiritual consciousness.

5. *Sufism & The Perennial Philosophy.* Aldous Huxley and others have written on the Perennial Philosophy which suggests there is an underlying unity, or internal connectedness, to all the great religions. The world's great religions are united through this inner, primordial spiritual energy; often, it is the outward expression which changes and is different according to time, place and culture.

Further, it is through this internal unifying energy that the spiritual traveler connects and unites with Ultimate Truth. Over the centuries, some have termed this way of learning and experiencing Ultimate Truth mysticism.

Islam through its mystical branch, Sufism, is the world's most recent major projection of this ancient way of spiritual learning. Yet, all religions have available at their very center the experience of Ultimate Truth; this inner spiritual way of learning is the path of the spiritual traveler, and is available to everyone all of the time.

Further, this path existed long before Islam or Sufism and may be experienced in ordinary life, independent of Sufism. For the spiritual traveler, Sufism and this ancient way of perceiving ultimate reality are one and the same. While many of the quotes and references are Sufi ones- similar views, quotes, and inner spiritual experiences are available through all spiritual and religious traditions.

One of the first lessons taught in the mystical school is how to monitor daily thoughts and feelings. Isn't it amazing how many thoughts and feelings pass through our bodies and minds on a daily basis? Did you ever stop to consider this? Gradually, through monitoring personal thoughts and feelings and recognizing patterns, along with guidance from the teacher on how to examine the underlying assumptions behind these patterns, the spiritual traveler learns to master fluctuations of consciousness, being able to sift through and quiet them; in order to connect with what lies beyond daily awareness. While some feelings and thoughts are enjoyable and easier to push aside than bothersome ones, the spiritual traveler, through practice, at specific times, must be able to still all thoughts and feelings. The assumption being that once this is done, the awareness deep within, beyond daily cares, can be awakened. This is the mystical process, pushing aside daily thoughts and feelings, in order to connect with our own inner higher consciousness.

Like a television remote, we learn to work the channels in our mind, so we can easily go to the designated setting that plays "higher consciousness." There is a Middle Eastern joke figure, Mulla Nasrudin, who illustrates how he has mastered and in part made his thoughts work for him.

> Mulla Nasrudin was visiting his psychiatrist. Among the many questions the doctor asked was: "Are you bothered by improper thoughts" "Not at all," said Nasrudin. "The truth is I rather enjoy them."

In the next section, like Nasrudin, we begin to play the different stations in our mind and make them work for us. For most travelers, these are the voices of competing streams that automatically come on to help us:

7

- when we have a presenting problem

- an important question to answer

- or, a matter of conscience to consider.

In our dialogue, the higher consciousness or part that knows the answers to the questions we ask ourselves speaks using italics. In part, this is the awareness that the spiritual traveler seeks to awaken and further develop. The everyday mind, which is needed to function in the world, offers the questions, and "speaks" in regular print. This is the part that must be quieted and stilled so the higher consciousness can come forward and answer. By asking questions and helping us through life, the everyday mind does its job, so, the higher consciousness, under the right circumstances, can operate and lead us higher.

\*      \*

# Our First "Conversation" – Life is all About Me!

So what you're saying is that for the most part, this life is about me. While what I do is connected and may be important to others, in the final analysis, it is all about me; now, do I have this right?

*Pretty much.*

So many religious philosophies talk about giving to others, helping your fellow man, and we are all one, connected spiritually, in the eyes of God. So if we take care of ourselves, aren't we taking care of everyone? I'm having trouble reconciling the two concepts because, from my background in psychology, I know that researchers have found that even in giving, humans are helping themselves. In effect, there is no such thing as true altruism. Then, why is there so much emphasis, from a religious and spiritual perspective, on helping and doing right for others?

*Because it is part of our basic human, social obligation, living in a larger community, to help our neighbor; it is a requirement of being a human being and part of the job of all religion is to set-up foundational social and moral values. Also, spiritually, by helping others, for the most part, we are helping our self reach our personal highest potential; a selfish-altruistic form of expression.*

Selfish-altruism- come again? When I help another, I help myself; how does that work?

*Because when your neighbor is hungry or suffering, you are hungry and suffering. On a spiritual level, we are all one. And since we are all one, life is about me and "us" at the same time.*

I've heard that one before, but it is pretty difficult to make that work on a practical, every day, personal level. Let alone understand it totally and feel what you are talking about.

*From a social perspective, here's an example. If your neighbor is hungry and is suffering, their pain and desperation may cause them to steal, hurt another or commit a crime. In turn, this raises local insurance rates, people become generally fearful and you may even have an item taken from your own home. Also, in some parts of the world, the hungry and desperate, in exchange for food and self-esteem are being taught their enemy is anyone who doesn't believe, in a religious sense, as they do. In exchange for needed food, they are being used and manipulated into becoming killing machines; being used to further selfish plans of individual power brokers. It's interesting to note that suicide bombers rarely come from wealthy or politically influential families but from poor ones.*

*Additionally, research of volunteers indicates that for the most part, volunteers who help as little as 3 hours a week are both physically and mentally happier than their counterparts who do not volunteer. Scientists are starting to suspect that somehow helping others sets off biochemical properties in the brain and body that contribute to our overall health and well being.*

OK. I'm starting to get it ... So to help another might also help my overall health and the general well being of the community around me. Now, to go back to the original discussion, you mean that most of the spiritual learning and personal expression, in this life, are basically for myself; not others ... not even my family.

*Pretty much.*

That's tough to wrap my head around. Life is all about me, but isn't my family a part of me?

*If it will help, let's go back to the beginning of your life. Now, why did you come here?*

As I understand, I came to this life to experience, create, work, learn and serve.

*Yes. That is correct. We all come here to express who we are, and the highest expression of anyone's "self," spiritually, is to help others. We are equipped with certain skills and abilities that assist in the development of our highest expression. Along our spiritual path, we face specific experiences, which challenge us and serve to further our development. In giving of ourselves and helping our neighbors, we move forward to a higher realization of self.*

> Beyond words and desires
> There is an underlying Reality
> Which unifies all things.
> This Reality
> And the method to perceive it
> Is the birthright of humanity.
>
> In their journey through this world
> Most people become distracted
> And fixate on all manner of things.
> In a sense, these things
> Then become their reality
> And they have no need of anything higher.

S.B.

So, my experiences with the spiritual schools and the different ways of learning happened to help me unlock what was already inside, so, I could eventually help others?

*For the most part, that is correct.*

I still don't get it, if it's mostly about me, how are we all connected? It seems like a total contradiction.

*When the mind questions, the heart or soul answers. On one level, we have discussed this with the example of the hungry neighbor who is turned into a criminal or terrorist. Yet, you have to **perceive** the connection with your own inner spiritual capacity. The real or lasting answer is not thought out: it is perceived or known by another part of self.*

Another part of myself? How many "selves" do I have anyway?

*Throughout our lives we experience many selves and that is the point of the different social roles we play. Some examples include, father, lover, hospital worker, writer, teacher, little league coach and member of a bowling team. However, for our present conversation and this book there are basically two, the part that questions, and the part that knows the answers.*

It always comes down to that spiritual knowing doesn't it?

*Yes. It does. But remember spiritual knowing is natural and really not that difficult or complicated. Similar to how you know you are in love. People will ask, "How did you know?" Well, one day, after spending hours with your beloved, you just knew. Remember, you are a multi-level being with many levels of understanding and knowing, that need to be expressed in daily life.*

It's just not easy to operate on a day-to-day basis that way. We live on this earth with other "regular" people and somehow have to deal with "regular" concerns. These "regular" concerns are annoying, take time, energy and often it's hard to see the connection between the everyday and the more dramatic spiritual stuff.

*Who said this was going to be easy? All the "regular" stuff has its spiritual purpose, too. What good is spiritual learning if it isn't put into practice in daily life? That's why we undergo all that preparation and learning. To help self and others realize the connection between the everyday and spiritual. When the young mother suckles her babe in the middle of the night, how is this not an act of spiritual love? Or when the parent, at the crack of dawn commutes long distances to work to provide for their family? Always, it is a matter of intention, a gentle love song we sing to help others.*

Yes. Yes. I know it's my job to help others through this writing, and that's part of the reason I came to this life, but do you think anyone will believe any of this?

*Does it really matter? This is about you remember, what you have to experience and express. Because in your highest expression, as we all are connected, everyone benefits.*

But I am so tired of writing things that a limited number of people read; and editors give me a hard time with. This material is so important, and must be shared; yet it just doesn't seem to fit the expected mold. I guess I'm just waiting for the part where "everyone benefits" and it seems to be taking a really long time.

*So. You want to complain. Remember what your mother used to say, the complaint department is on the sixth floor (and in the building where you lived there were only five floors).*

Sure, I remember; she was something.

*She still is ...*

OK. Now, let's get back to the subject at hand... which is? I forget.

*Your next book or, as it is more accurate to say, everyone's next book. Because we are all one ... remember? It might be worth describing and explaining our spiritual philosophy, as we understand it. Maybe elaborate a little more on how we came to the conclusion that life is all about "me." What do you think?*

OK. I'll give it a shot ... we're calling this book **Sufism for Western Seekers**, right?

*Yes, that's what we're calling it. A <u>Conversations With God</u>, by Neale Donald Walsch knock-off kind of a thing ... building off of his great idea, and hopefully reaching as many people as he did with our own message.*

Do you think anyone will notice?

*Sure, but who cares? We're all one right? So, since we are working on the book, and are putting the time and effort into making it something that will help others, "someone" has already noticed, don't you think?*

Sure, but it's getting our editor to notice that's really the first challenge.

*Touché.*

To continue to explain our philosophy, basically we are all spiritual beings who have come into the earth phase to experience our selves, create and do all kinds of wondrous things. Because of the physical, special nature of this earthly realm, we have the capacity to create and freely choose many opportunities. This capacity to freely choose and create makes us, excuse the term, god-like. Each of us has a spiritual aspect within that is most like the Divine; in our truest essence we are all sons and daughters of a King and travel through many worlds, experiencing and co-creating our own individual reality. In part, this comprises the larger reality, which we experience and help create on many different levels.

*Not bad for a beginning. Now get down to the individual, specific life.*

Each person or soul comes here with a life plan or set of things it wishes or needs to experience and accomplish; these things are freely chosen and are not imposed; they are part of a larger design. Most often, the specific aspects to our life plan are hidden deep within our soul, unfold over time and come to consciousness as feelings or ideas; for example, a deep knowing, I feel strongly this is something I need to do. Usually, we bring with us a skill set, temperament, and enjoyment of specific activities that help us accomplish our goals. Everyone has talents and skills for all sorts of things. In the short run, some of our life experiences may be viewed as painful but in the long run are aspects of the specific design into which the soul has chosen to participate. For example, a painful beating death like my younger brother's was part of the larger experience of who he was and what he was to accomplish and experience in his lifetime. Sometimes, in order to move forward we need to experience, what on one level is 'called' painful; yet, from a larger perspective is all part of the one and leads to a higher aspect or realization of self. Consider the drunk who can only come to true spiritual realization after years of drinking and self-destruction. Hitting rock bottom, so to speak, is sometimes necessary before any form of growth or enlightenment can occur.

> Enlightenment must come little by little- otherwise it would overwhelm.
>
> Idries Shah

*That's good for a start. Let's elaborate a bit on our younger brother's spiritual journey so that the reader can understand what we just explained more clearly.*

OK. It's not easy to share this with everyone, but I hope that in sharing our readers will begin to understand our spiritual philosophy a bit more clearly.

## Don't Go to San Francisco

One day, I introduced my young brother Ben to Sam, my teacher in the mystical school. At the time, Ben was an aspiring musician and felt his best musical opportunities would be in San Francisco. After a few visits, Sam cautioned Ben that he shouldn't go to San Francisco and that he should stay in New York City with the people who loved him. Sam indicated that Ben could pursue his musical career in New York as well as continue his spiritual studies here.

Ben eventually left for San Francisco. Later, when I asked Sam why he cautioned against this move, Sam indicated he saw a dark cloud around Ben there; and if Ben stayed here he would be protected by his family and the Light. Sam said, his spiritual Light extended only so far and he feared for Ben in San Francisco.

As the years turned to decades, Sam's warning came to pass and Ben did not meet with the overall outcome of success he sought. Initially, Ben's music was successful, but this was short lived. In fact, it was a very difficult time for Ben that saw a gradual, lengthy decline in overall health, drug use, and his eventual brutal death on the streets.

How Sam was able to look into the future and know that dark clouds faced Ben, at the time, I was unsure. Also, that experience made me stop and think if I were faced with this decision, would I have done the same thing? Would I have changed my plans, based upon a warning by a man I just met? How many of us would have done that? Yet, the warning was given and ignored by my brother whose soul chose to participate in a specific sequence of events.

So, again, the important lesson to take from Ben's story is not that he should have listened to Sam, but that he had to follow his spiritual path in his lifetime. People might think, "What a senseless way to live and die." But as counter productive as it may seem, Ben needed to experience what he did in his lifetime in order to move forward along the Path.

Yes, when we leave this place, we journey on to the next place and adventure. For some, it may be a return to the earth phase and for others, there are countless worlds and dimensions to experience. Literally, we are spiritual travelers, going and doing; creating and destroying; all in the name of the Light- expressing ourselves in countless varied forms until we return to our true home and reign alongside the Light. This can be accomplished in an instant or over a hundred lifetimes. It can be accomplished once or over and over again. The great cycle of life continues to turn, and spiritually, with the proper perspective, we can do whatever we like; we are all creators, who each moment, join in creating our personal reality. And this includes all of the day-to-day "regular" stuff as well as the "big picture" stuff too.

*Not bad. You're making a lot of progress. Now let's continue to explain the importance of an individual approach in spiritual studies. Over time in the mystical school, while most of the sessions were in a small group, in order for the impact to take effect, the learning had to be specific to the student. The following story about our spiritual group's attendance at a conference illustrates one example of how individual teaching was offered. Can you talk about what happened that day?*

Sure. This is an example of the kind of thing that happened all the time with Sam.

## Individual Approach to Learning

We had just come out of a professional presentation about the use of healthy pleasures (Robert Ornstein, *Healthy Pleasures*) in every day life. Happiness and better health being achieved through seemingly minor daily activities: looking forward to and eating our favorite food, watching that new, exciting TV show, or the first anticipated cup of coffee in the morning; with most people's happiness being made up of countless small pleasures and events. The big events, for most people, like a wedding, new car, or a promotion were few and far between, and not the source of the greatest daily pleasures in life.

I remarked to Sam, who suggested our group of students attend; this approach could be very helpful for depressed patients, and would be useful in the delivery of therapeutic recreation services. At which point, Sam remarked, "You miss the point: this approach is for the individual."

In time, I came to understand that while this approach to happiness and health could help groups of people, always, the orientation needed to be on the individual; the group was made up of individuals. It is the same with spiritual studies. The world is made a better place, one person at a time, by participating in spiritual growth and development. In this way, the whole world benefits from the actions of each individual.

## Sam Saying

Sam used to say that most people deluded themselves by striving for happiness or peace. Both of these conditions were transitory and couldn't be maintained. What people should strive to reach was God- God was all that was permanent.

*What do you say we give our readers an exercise; something practical to do that will help them connect with this material?*

Sounds good - that's what helped us get started in the beginning, when we were still so full of questions.

## Daily Activity: Quiet, Alone Time

*Daily, each traveler should set aside 10-20 minutes to travel inward. This is personal time where the external noise of the world can be turned*

18

*off and an examination of the many parts of self may be conducted. We need to go over the days events and examine our thoughts and reactions.*

*The emphasis on the identification of troubling thoughts, reactions and improve upon them- by reacting differently or substituting different thought patterns. If we have made a mistake, try to correct it and move forward. Even busy mothers or executives must be selfish about this, and take the time to do something for self. Some travelers do this at day's end and others wake up early; some have time during their lunch hour and others by going for a walk after dinner. Over time, we must recognize the many selves so we can push them aside for a time, and unlock what lies beyond daily consciousness. Going inward may be accomplished through prayer, journaling, meditation, or at day's end observing the repeating patterns of thought.*

\*     \*

## — 4 —

# Our Conversation Continues – Hunger Pains that Can't Be Cured with Food...

The sight of someone eating will not appease your hunger. The spiritual experience of others cannot satisfy your yearning.

Traditional

Another day and we are back at it. How long do you think this conversation will go on?

*It's pretty hard to tell. Until we finish, I guess.*

How long do you think that will take? You know we are just taking shots in the dark; there is no commitment from anyone that this will get published or even see the light of day.

*Yes. I understand that, but sometimes you just have to take a chance, make things up as you go along and trust yourself. Also, publication and recognition is not what this is about. Correct? Or have you forgotten the reason for all of this?*

No. I haven't forgotten, but it wouldn't hurt to let them know.

*You write because you have to write. You have a message to share and what happens with it is not completely up to you. In the doing is the joy.*

*Like a songbird in the forest that serenades the rising sun, caring not if another hears her notes. Remember, in the singing is the joy. In our case, in the writing is the joy.*

OK. Very poetic, but it's pretty hard to pay bills with joy and no funds; singing without an audience.

*You know, you really are a complainer.*

Yes. I know. I can't help it; it's the New York City-Jewish thing.

*Are we ready to go on?*

OK. We were discussing our spiritual philosophy, correct?

> This is the original religion before there was religion: it is a path of spiritual learning and love. Religion is a highway to take you to the door. Love of God and your own spiritual capacity unlock and lead you through it.

S.B.

As you know, in order for life to have real meaning you must feel passionately about something- I was a songbird looking for my own special song. The 'great emptiness or hunger' was pushing me onward.

*Hmmm... 'great hunger' - I think you better further explain the concept to our readers who may have never heard of this traditional term.*

Within each person there is an 'empty space' or 'great hunger' that is waiting to be filled by the 'Light of God;' this emptiness manifests as an unease, fear or ache. This unease, pain or hunger drives people onward, seeking to fill this void with all kinds of things. Some fill this empty space by working excessively; others by attaching themselves to a cause; some by engaging in excessive and

21

destructive habits like drugs, alcohol, and gambling, gossiping or sexual addiction.

   The search for ways to fill the emptiness stops when the traveler realizes the 'real or lasting goal' of life on this Earth, which is higher expression of self and service to God. Once this happens, then true living and work begin.

> The world is a giant bazaar.
> A marketplace where you will find
> Exactly what you are seeking.
> If you seek garbage it is there.
> Similarly if you desire sweets
> And sensory experience
> There are many vendors.
>
> Blessed is the shopper
> Who knows what to purchase.
> Unfortunately most leave
> Without making the right choice.

S.B.

*Are you implying from a spiritual perspective, the early part of your life that seemed to make little sense was a preparation for the moment of awakening?*

   It's pretty hard to generalize that much about the first 25 years of my life. Certainly, there were people and experiences I felt deeply about. I loved my wife and family; I enjoyed sports, physical exercise and by that time had found an occupation I enjoyed, yet, inwardly, there was still a deep, personal restlessness and unease that the religion of my birth could not quiet. I needed something more that I could not name. I came to realize that the Light could satisfy my hunger in ways that I never dreamed possible. In fact, had I not experienced this indescribable hunger, I would not have been able to participate in the type of learning that the mystical school offered.

*Really? You need to explain why that is...*

Well, a prerequisite for this type of learning and experience through the teacher is an inner burning or hunger for Truth, which we've just discussed. While the traveler may not even be aware that the unease which he/she experiences is a hunger for things of the spirit; at some point, the traveler must accept that it was this inborn unease, friction and burning which pushed them on to search for the missing piece. Additionally, this learning and experience must be sought for itself; not for its rewards or what it will bring personally. This is termed 'sincerity' and must already be present; again, this capacity may be refined, but cannot be given to the traveler. The teacher is able to perceive these inner capacities in the traveler, and at the proper time, calls. That is why the age-old injunction is true, that when the student is ready the teacher appears. It is precisely the traveler's *desire* for spiritual experience, with a teacher, that blocks the teacher's appearance. During the course of spiritual learning, strong emotions like desire must be suspended, and the student must have the inner capacity to sort out levels of personal motivation and quiet this inner noise. Again, the teacher can help the traveler refine this capacity however, before acceptance it must already exist within the traveler at a level it can be worked with.

*Hopefully, our fellow travelers aren't intimidated by such prerequisites!*

They shouldn't be. It's all inside, and happens naturally. There is a flow or synchronicity to it all. Let me share a story about my brother Paul and a friend of his that illustrates this point.

## Spiritual Search

While in their early twenties, my middle brother Paul and one of his friends, Joe, undertook a spiritual search for a teacher that took them across Asia and India. Heroically, Paul and Joe backpacked across thousands of miles searching for a holy man who could put them on the path to truth and enlightenment.

They searched for months in Tibet and India; and from their perspective were unsuccessful. After his odyssey, when I met Paul he told me a story of something that happened in India which helped send him back to the states. As Paul put it, it really pissed him off to travel thousands of miles, and get this for an answer.

Paul and Joe entered a small town in India and made some inquiries about the local holy men. Finally, through persistence and a local interpreter, they were able to gain an audience with these men. When taken to the temple, Paul and Joe saw before them a number of bearded old men who were sitting and praying. Quickly, they were brought before the youngest looking man, who through the interpreter asked, why they had come. Paul answered, to find a holy man who could teach them of Truth. Next, the holy man asked Paul what he had in his backpack. Paul took out some of the books he was carrying, a variety of metaphysical discourses, and explained through the interpreter what was in these books. As the holy man leafed through these books, he looked at Paul and Joe and questioned, 'Sadhu?' Again, he pointed at them both and repeated in a questioning tone, 'Sadhu,' following that up with a couple of rushed sentences.

Paul asked the interpreter what this all meant, and he said, "Sadhu means holy man; also, he has asked you both to leave immediately before you ruin the scam they have going on here with the other westerners." When Paul and Joe understood what the bearded one meant, angrily, they gathered up their books and left. Here Paul and Joe had traveled thousands of miles looking for a holy man, and when they had finally met some, they were told they were holy men and asked to leave. Paul wanted instruction, not to be told he was his own teacher.

When Paul returned to New York City, I introduced him to Sam and Paul's spiritual journey took a different direction. He sat with Sam and learned what he had traveled thousands of miles to find. Ironically, it was waiting for him in the city of his birth.

Looking back, we all learned something from this story and adventure. No matter how hard you try, unless it is the right time, in the right place, with the right people, a teaching situation will not occur. Also, it may be in the place you least expect- your own back yard.

In some ways, the Indian holy man was correct; we are our own 'Sadhu.' We have within, the answer to our questions, and are awaiting the right conduit.

*So the right conduit awaits the specific student. For learning to occur, always, it is a matter of right time, right place, and right people. Is there anything else travelers should know about admittance into a mystical school or course of study?*

Well, in some mystical schools, after acceptance, the student has to wait a preparation period of 1001 days before entering into a formal course of study. In fact, the book title, *1001 Tales of the Arabian Nights*, derives from this tradition. In my case and that of others, we did not have to wait the prescribed period. Perhaps we were in desperate need of the teaching?

*From my perspective, I'd say the answer to that is a big "Yes!"*

You would! But seriously, before entering, some students are able to wait out the entire preparation period; we needed instruction immediately. In fact, there is a traditional story about this situation that has been repeated many times.

## Waiting Period

A new student petitioned for admission to a mystical school and was inquiring to the head student. The head student offered, the new fellow would only be admitted after passing a test. The head student posed a question and brought the new student's answer to the teaching master. The master sent word via the head student that the new fellow had answered the question correctly and should return in 1001 days to receive the teaching.

Puzzled the new student inquired, 'what would have happened if I answered the question incorrectly?" The head student replied, 'Oh then, you would have been admitted right way.'

*Talk more about how traditional religion can fit in with or complement the spiritual traveler's journey toward the Light.*

Sure. In the mystical school, Sam never told us to follow this creed or that religion. What he said was that if you followed the path and were a servant of God, you would become a better Christian, Muslim or Jew. The religion of your birth was more or less an accident, and as you progressed along the path, you would embrace your own religion that much more. It wasn't until I had been studying with Sam for 3 years or so that I learned he was a Muslim. A friend told me this and we began to read the Koran. Sam never instructed us to do this. It just happened; and as I became familiar with the Koran and other books of the great religions, I came to see that they are all joined in the Light of Truth.

Here's another activity that will help spiritual travelers see the connection between traditional religious teaching and progress toward their own higher destiny.

## Daily Activity: Good Deeds

*Daily, do something positive, generous, or helpful for another person; do just one thing. Try to perform this good deed secretly without the person knowing. If they find out -that's OK- we wish to minimize indebtedness where the recipient feels they owe something in return. Make a list of good deeds or positive actions that you want to accomplish for others. In performing this positive activity, the good feelings you generate will be your reward and the energy attached to your feelings gradually will change you. If you no longer need to do these things to help you feel better than do these things for others and the higher destiny. By making your actions an offering, you will be joining in the higher destiny and consciously moving along the path.*

## Sam Saying

Religion is the basis of life. It is the focus from which all other things spring.

\*       \*

# Our Conversation Continues – Sufism and the Mystical School Begin to Ease the Great Hunger

The purpose of Sufi study and development of "being" is, among other things, the establishment and maintenance of a way of thinking and perception which prevents the recurrence of primitive thought and action (including the predominance of the reward/punishment mechanism and indoctrination) instead of merely having secondary aspirations, as with all other institutions, however fundamental, or even vital, these may be.

Abdul-Wahab T. Tiryaqi

*For those readers who have never been in a mystical school or even thought about being in one, what would you like to share about your time there and learning experience? If we were to summarize a few things other travelers need to know for their own adventures on the Path, what would those be?*

That's a pretty full question, if you know what I mean. It's hard to prioritize a "few things" when we all have so much to learn! Let me think about this a minute...

Say, before answering that question about the mystical school; I have one for you. Have you figured out where we are going with all of this?

*No. Not really. Thought we would make it up as we went along; like most of life you know, just wing it. Remember, while there are fixed points in each traveler's life; for the most part, life is something you make up as you go along. Moment by moment, the traveler creates their own consciousness, reality, and movement through the worlds. In each moment, there is opportunity for personal excellence.*

That's what I thought. Great.

*Now, there's no reason to get hostile. Are you ready?*

Sure. But before I do that, let me provide some background information. The teaching sessions themselves took place at work; the teacher, Sam was a psychiatrist born in Lahore, Pakistan whose father was a Sufi. At the time, I was working in a large, New York State psychiatric hospital, had just gotten married and, within the hospital, been transferred to a new unit. Additionally, I just enrolled at New York University, in a doctoral program, and the furthest thing from my mind was religion or spiritual learning. By this time, I realized spiritual learning was an important component of healthy living, however, I figured I'd get around to it sometime after I completed the doctorate. How often do we put off attending to our spiritual nature while we take care of "other things?"

As I worked at my new job, I became friendly with another staff member named Zach; over a few months time, we realized we had things in common like poetry and sports. We also shared the same desire for finding greater meaning in our lives. One day, Zach told me he had a spiritual teacher, and the teacher wanted to meet me. I was totally surprised and further intrigued when I learned this teacher worked right at the hospital. So the next day, we brought bag lunches and went to the teacher's office for an initial meeting, and what turned out to be my initiation to higher studies. I had no idea what to expect and didn't think I was looking for a spiritual experience. I couldn't even successfully meditate!

As the days passed into weeks and years, there were many lunchtime visits. Also, there were friends, relatives, and acquaintances that we introduced to the teacher. Sam was very gracious

and welcomed all visitors. Some of the visitors thought he was egotistical; others took what was offered, and still others quickly lost
interest. Each participant received the piece of the Teaching they
were meant to receive and continued on their Path.

> He that is purified by love; and he that is absorbed in
> the beloved and hath abandoned all else is a Sufi.

> Sirdar Ikbal Ali Shah

*OK, so now do you feel ready to share some of the most vibrant points
of the teaching with our fellow travelers?*

Looking back, I guess the number one thing I learned in the
mystical school was to love God, and that God was a living, loving,
vibrant, and creative element. Through direct perception, and the
teacher's intervention by reflecting the Light upon our hearts, we
experienced and became one with an entity or energy that seemed
to be the very life source of the universe. When you connected with
this energy; you knew and realized on an inner level that this was
your home and the Source. An aspect of this energy was already
inside of us, and this energy permeated the air, the desks, chairs,
and walls of the room. It was every place, and was the underlying
unity; it was the missing piece that quieted the great hunger, and
was the hidden treasure for which the mystics searched. All the
while, it was inside of us, waiting to be unlocked and fill us with
love and Light; setting our hearts aglow and lifting us up onto the
path.

*So somehow you felt a love so great that it made your emptiness go
away. Can you explain this a little more?*

Many people, when they think about encountering or having an
experience with God, envision somehow being with a mysterious,
happy, elderly, kind person in a pleasing setting. Because of the
wonderful energy of this situation, their feelings fill them with joy,

love and peace. Or perhaps, their vision involves a beautiful pastoral scene, friends, happy family, and music; all together sharing a peaceful afternoon meal, amidst a luxurious garden; this garden being the home of a loving, generous ruler who has invited them to celebrate. For the artist, poetic visions call forth an experience that goes beyond ordinary sensory awareness. William Blake writes about "seeing a world in a grain of sand" and Ralph Waldo Emerson of "singing the body electric."

In each vision, the outcome is profound feelings of love, bliss, happiness, peace and connection. In the beginning of the mystical path, there is a spiritual state called, "the oneness of creation experience;" where the traveler encounters the Light, or universal energy, and experiences their inner connection to every living thing; this spiritual experience is much like gently slipping deep below the peaceful waters of a quiet, cool, pool and slowly feeling yourself being absorbed and becoming one with the refreshing waters, fish and plants. Softly, as the water holds you in its embrace, miraculously, you still retain your individuality but at the same time, as you surrender to the water, become part of everything and feel safe; protected by something you cannot see, only feel. In today's drug oriented language, travelers might call this experience "getting high on God."

Often, when Sam guided us in meditation, we were embraced and engulfed by an energy that was pulsating, alive, peaceful, kind and all knowing. This universal energy Sam called the Light, because it dissipated spiritual darkness and united with our individual consciousness and expanded it outward, into all four directions at once; during that time, there was no time or space; no up or down and we rode on this wave of pure energy, love and Light through the cosmos. During this time, it seemed as if we were everywhere all at once; because of this loving, kind energy we realized we were safe, eternal and nothing could permanently harm us.

It was the power of this experience that lifted me up and filled me with so much spiritual love, that it altered the course of my life. During those sessions, where we were initiated and caressed by this energy, somehow I remembered my eternal connection with this life energy and became One with its loving embrace.

At that moment, I realized that God had always been concerned and had come looking for me. Over the years, my cup was empty so God could fill it. And during my initiation to this energy, for the first time, I heard the inner voice whisper: "I was loved, and God had always existed." It was then I made the inner promise to spend the rest of my life seeking God and celebrating this love.

*Wow - that was profound and beautiful, if you don't mind me saying. Now, let's get back to what else you learned in the school. And yes, there is even more to tell, isn't there?*

Indeed, you know I could write a book about this stuff! We also learned that we were multi-dimensional souls who came into this experience to use all aspects of consciousness, talent, and skills to help make this world better. We were urged to be like the river that gives to all travelers: some will come to drink because they were thirsty; others will come to dump their garbage; some will come to take a boat across the river; others will wish to journey the river to its source. Our job was to give to all without question and continue flowing; it was not the job of the river to question or make judgments about individual motivation.

One day, Sam made the statement that if this teaching was being presented in a different country it would be mind to mind. In our western culture, what was required was that the teaching be presented using questions and answers. Here, the travelers or students needed a verbal interchange. The underlying message was the same no matter what the format of the teaching. The energy or Light which called to our inner soul; this was the life fabric or spiritual juice to it all. Along with this point of view came the teaching and inner realization that all the religions were extensions of the Light. Across time, geography, and culture, religion varied because people were different, yet, on an inner level, united; it was this inner level or mystical experience that we drank from daily. For all people, this inner connection was on a deeply unconscious level and through training could be brought to full consciousness, as required. It was this inner connection that gave our soul its life energy.

## Activity: Giving to Others

*Part of healthy, balanced living and ordinary social duty is being part of a family or community, contributing, working and giving to others. If you have time, volunteer once a week at the local hospital, or nightly help your children do their homework. Perhaps listen to the problems of a co-worker or neighbor, join the local food pantry or routinely give to your favorite charity. The activity of giving should be entered into freely, anonymously if possible, without resentment or repeated troubling thoughts like: people tell me I need to do this. If you cannot do this without displeasure, wait until you can. Then observe the many benefits.*

## Sam's Religion

The religion Sam followed was a simple one. It was love of God and service to humanity. The point of religion was to make a more complete traveler who would be of better service to others. Sam stated that his business was not making converts and handing out mystical states, but of making better travelers who loved God. This religion had always existed and would always exist. It was the inner path of all the religions and he was just a servant doing his job.

\*       \*

# Our Conversation Continues – Sufis are Everyday People Living Life as a Prayer

The Hoopoe continued: The next valley is the Valley of Love. To enter it one must be a flaming fire- what shall I say? A man must himself be fire. The face of the lover must be enflamed, burning and impetuous as fire. True love knows no after-thoughts; with love, good and evil cease to exist.

Attar

*Are we ready to get back to writing? You have been gone a few days.*

Maybe?

*What do you mean maybe? Isn't that what we agreed to do?*

Yes. It is, but things get in the way. You know life ... eating, working, shopping, cleaning and the everyday activity of living.

*You bring up an interesting point.*

Which is?

*How does this writing fit into everyday, ordinary life? What is the potential usefulness?*

You want me to explain or are you handling this?

*I'll handle it; this will give you more time to rest your tired self.*

Are we being sarcastic?

*Nah. Just stating the obvious. To continue, spirituality or religion is intended to become the center of a life; a place from which other things come forward. In life, there are many things to do; we are multi-dimensional beings having all kinds of interests, obligations and ways to express the self.*
    *First things first. Is it spiritual or good sense to have young children calling out for help selecting their school clothing or bills waiting to get paid, because we are sitting in the room praying? Probably not. From our perspective, the best thing would be to turn helping the children dress, and working extra hours to pay the bills into our prayer.*

Say again?

*You know what I am talking about.*

Yeah, but they're going to think you're crazy! Praying is something most people go to church to do. For the reader who may not know about intention, please elaborate.

*As you know, from our point of view, prayer and ordinary life are entwined. The goal of spiritual studies is to make life the prayer; every action an expression of our higher self and the higher destiny of the universe. Something we do for God and to help make the world a little better place. So, when I help my children get ready for school in the morning, I do this consciously to help make them better prepared so they can go out into the world and make it better. With every action, I am dedicating this activity to the greater good or Light. As I help them select their clothes, potentially, this is the song that is in my heart and becomes my higher intention. The goal of the spiritual traveler is to bring this focus more and more into conscious daily living.*

How beautiful.

*Yes, it is. Now are you ready to continue?*

OK. Picking up on the theme of everyday activity as spiritual practice or prayer; this was another lesson learned in the school. Through the prayer of submission and experiencing submission of everyday thoughts and ego into the Light, we learned about alignment with the higher self. This alignment is not a static condition; it comes and goes- depending upon external circumstances and what is going on in our lives.

> No matter anyone's fancy philosophy, don't let them fool you: life is a multi-level experience and a full-contact sport. Inside this arena, there are plenty of ups and downs; yet, far below the surface there is peaceful tranquility and the One.

S.B.

## Sam Saying

If you're going to be happy, be happy with God.
Similarly, if you're going to be sad, be sad with God.

If I am busy vacuuming, the kids are yelling, and the phone is ringing, it is impossible to center my self and dedicate my actions to something higher. I am trying to survive in that moment, yet, on another day, I may be able to offer up a prayer that dedicates this activity of caring for my family to the Light. Remember, we were meant to be in the world and hold a part of ourselves 'sacred;'

remaining internally focused on the Light. The journey is to bring this latent, or inner, hidden spirituality forward by consciously aligning everyday thoughts with our spiritual awareness.

*So what you are saying is that we need to forgive ourselves in the moments when the "small stuff" seems to overwhelm us into ego-driven thoughts and actions, and just try to regain our internal focus to let our spiritual nature come forward. Since it's inside of us, it's the most natural thing in the world.*

Yes! But letting it happen is easier said than done. That's why the need for a school and a teacher along the Path.

> Each traveler is a link in an unbroken chain that extends far into the distant past and stretches into the emerging future. One of countless- calling the name of God throughout the ages.

S.B.

So let's explain about the Sufis. Who are they? What do they teach and who are their students?

*As you know, but our readers may not, Sufis do not call themselves Sufis. There are a number of reasons for this, some of which include:*

- *The term itself did not appear until the late 1800's and was derived from the woolen (Soof) robes worn by certain ascetics in the middle, eastern part of the world.*

- *According to tradition, this ancient way of spiritual learning, and experiencing the Light, has existed since the beginning; before there was organized religion. Our teacher called it the original superhighway to God, because this form of learning could accomplish in one lifetime what typically took 3 or 4 lifetimes.*

- *According to other teachers, Sufism was not a doctrine that was thought out, nor written about, or even discussed; while travelers often did all of these things- it was a primordial 'essence' or 'attitude' which was learned and experienced in the company of other Sufis. Idries Shah called it something that was perceived by an "organ of inner awareness."*

- *To call one self a Sufi is arrogant; it is the end product of a form of spiritual learning. Followers of this path, typically call themselves seeker, traveler or dervish; one who is continuing to travel and learn.*

- *Finally, according to one of my teachers, this knowledge was the secret doctrine taught in the mystery schools of the ancient pyramids. Targeting personal excellence, it is the original human development system through which the world becomes a better place, one person at a time.*

- *Further, it is believed that each person is unique, and the outcome of this learning varies according to surrounding need, and individual destiny or life plan.*

- *Students can come from any walk of life, religion or spiritual background. It is expected that the student exhibit or have a level of what is called 'sincerity;' this being an inner truthfulness which seeks the teaching for itself and not for personal gain.*

*Some people call the Sufis the original mystics, and Idries Shah in his 'ground breaking' book,* The Sufis, *traces numerous spiritual and metaphysical systems to this ancient tradition. Accordingly, all the great religions and spiritual systems are linked by an inner current or energy that is the underlying fabric of the universe. It is this force, or Light, that the Sufi learns to perceive and use in everyday life; this force, or Logos in other traditions, is an enriching and enabling element that is unifying, holistic and life enhancing. Within, we all have an aspect of this wondrous element termed 'the heart,' which is our spiritual center; this is the center which enables and directs all physical, mental, emotional and spiritual life. When our body dies, it is this part which leads the soul on to the next place.*

*People forget or simply are not taught that spiritual teachings and religions vary according to time and place. Also, they vary by cultural and sociological needs of people in the receiving part of the world. This is the external form, or clothing that surrounds the teaching. Internally, all forms are one; and just like we require garments for hot and cold, wet and dry, so, the religious form has shifted according to the people's need.*

So that explains why there is really one Truth, but so many "different" forms of it in the various world religions. What is it that the Sufis do exactly?

*Followers of this tradition have jobs just like every one else, while performing many different and varied hidden spiritual functions; according to tradition, one of these functions is that there is a hierarchy of Sufis who are guardians of the plan for humanity, daily reflecting the Light into the world. Without this Light all life would quickly wither and die.*

*Travelers for the most part are integrated into the fabric of their community, have families and social duties like everyone else. Early on, they are taught that spiritual duties were in addition to responsibilities of daily life. Throughout history, travelers on this path, or lovers of God, have been mothers, ascetics, generals, kings, physicians, shepherds, and great religious leaders. Many travel anonymously, unknown to the general public; this lack of public awareness protects them, and every town and community has these people. They are the person next door, ordinary in appearance; with work to do in this world, and their heart in the next world.*

What will people get from this form of learning?

*The object of this learning is a completed person. Someone who is balanced physically, emotionally, mentally and spiritually; able to use spiritual capacity in everyday life. In the past, these people were termed wise one, master, saint, and mystic. Over-achievers, people who were able to incorporate a measure of spirituality in daily life and help others around them reach higher.*

*Travelers who follow this path, some have termed extraordinary, or uniquely original, capable of spiritual sight and prescience; and because of individual spiritual capacity, in the past, may have been called heretics or put to death. Yet to the Sufi, these extraordinary capacities are natural, trained extensions of consciousness; available to anyone who is fitted through this training and learns to set free, spiritually, what is already inside them.*

How come I've never heard of the Sufis?

*In our western culture, this is not unusual. In Middle Eastern countries, Sufis are well known, revered, and even cultural icons. Through Islam, there has been a major Sufi projection with many current Sufi orders attributing their lineage to great Islamic spiritual teachers, saints and mystics.*

*As we have discussed, it is important to remember this way of learning pre-dates Islam; existed before there were religions, and is the inner core of spiritual learning. Because Islam is the last great religious form, it is perfectly natural that this projection has been used to convey the teaching. Traditionally, there is a mystical or experiential stream in Judaism, and Christianity; with many forms of Hinduism, Buddhism and Taoism emphasizing this aspect as well.*

*In the 1950's, there was a directed projection of this teaching into our western culture; which over the last 60 years has begun to mature. Interestingly enough, if you go to Amazon.com and search books for Sufi writings, 7000 (+) entries will display. This is just one indicator of their growing influence upon our western culture. Ever so slowly, this Sufi influence is becoming main stream. About five years ago, the number one selling poet in the United States was Rumi; universally acknowledged as one of the great mystical poets of all time. He is among the highest of Sufi Masters.*

I'd like to explain to our fellow travelers some of the reasons that it has thus far been difficult to study the Sufi system. According to Hoda Azizian it is due to two main factors:

- Learners select materials according to existing prejudices and do not know which are superseded or even spurious;

- Sufi learning is a comprehensive process (which has been called both 'holistic' and 'organic.') It cannot be studied from the outside at all without distortion.

Azizian continues to explain that within the Sufi system, we can isolate three areas which have to be represented and in balance. These are:

- The learner has to be attuned to the teacher and the teaching. This involves his achieving a balanced attitude: neither rejecting nor servile;

- The materials have to be present and 'sprinkled' (the technique known as scatter must be employed). They must bypass excess emotional or intellectual capacity.

- The energy and focus of the teaching must be right. This requires allowance for the cyclical nature of the availability of the necessary energy and the recipient's ability to absorb it.

## Daily Activity: Consciousness Building

*Daily in the beginning, each traveler needs to add consciousness expanding and focusing activities. One of the most familiar exercises of this type is meditation, because it teaches many things: skills like concentration, focus, and switching attention back to the focus word or object. If you have trouble meditating, try another activity, such as prayer or listening to quiet, peaceful music. These types of exercise may be learned from a book, class, or yoga teacher; for many it is part of the learning required, to still and push aside that which stands in our way. Usually, specific exercises are bridges to something else and as such, intended for fixed periods.*

## Sam Saying

Yes, it is good to have friends, family and a vocation. Of greater use is the realization of the One who gave these things to you.

\*       \*

41

# Our Conversation Continues – Discovering and Choosing Our Higher Selves in an Expectation & Rewards Kind of World

One night when the Sheikh Bayazid went out from the town he noticed that a profound silence lay over the plain. The moon lighted the world making the night as bright as day. The stars clustered according to their sympathies, and each constellation had its specific function. The sheikh walked on without seeing any movement or a single soul. His heart was stirred and he said: 'Lord, a piercing sadness moves me. Why is it that a court so sublime is without eager worshippers?' 'Be not amazed,' an inner voice answered, 'the King does not admit everyone to his court. His dignity does not suffer him to receive tramps at his door. When the sanctuary of our splendor sheds its effulgence it disdains the sleepy and heedless. You are one of a thousand who crave admission and you must wait patiently.'

Attar

*Good morning.*

No comedy today?

*Nah. Let's just get down to it.*

OK. Are you doing the talking or am I?

*I need to get things started. Before continuing with the material learned in the mystical school; let us divert a little and go back to the initial point at which we began this set of reflections: basically, this whole experience of life, while occurring simultaneously on a hundred different levels, when it comes down to it, is basically about us.*

*Each soul comes into the earth phase of life to experience all sorts of things and be a co-creator each moment along with the Light. In each moment that is quickly lived and then ends, each person has the opportunity to rise higher and create something. Each thought, action, and desire is an expression of self, and to take this energy which arises in the soul and place it into a form of intention, and then accomplish it, in effect pulling experience towards us, makes us co-creators.*

So we're co-creating our reality with thoughts, desires, and action?

*Yes, and each time we consciously create something, in the name of the Light, God rejoices. This is one of the highest expressions available in the earth phase; the other is doing something out of love for another and freely giving of one's self. When we extend our hand to help another who has fallen down, and offer this assistance in the name of God, we turn personal intention and everyday activity into living prayer. Because of the conscious focus on God and the higher energy vibration of giving, routine daily activity becomes something higher.*

*This is important to explain to our readers as an anchor or frame of reference. Many are probably questioning, "Can I really be a co-creator of my own reality?" The concept is not easy to wrap one's head around. It also endows our fellow travelers with a great deal of personal responsibility and accountability for how they conduct themselves on a day-to-day basis. So, how were you trained to align personal action, in creating something that was desired, with the Higher Destiny?*

I guess you're asking me a question, right? OK. I'll pick up from here.

In some of our exercises we were taught how to surrender our ego or daily consciousness so the higher part of self, which is you, essentially, could come forward. It was this aspect of our soul that was always aligned with God. When this aspect of consciousness was operating, we were reaching higher and our desire or thought was aligned with the Light; hence our own desire or thought was also the desire of the Light. Our consciousness became a stage across which the Light operated. We had surrendered a part of self and united with the higher, so in effect our intention was the same intention of the Light. Consequently, our resulting experience, which was about us, was, in effect, about the Light. Our consciousness, through the alchemy of love and spirit, became the consciousness, for a time, of the Light. At that precise moment, we were an instrument of the highest.

When we were shown God, in the form of universal energy that was reflected across our hearts, we were changed. As a result of contact with this energy our consciousness was altered or alchemized into something higher. This Light or energy that engulfed and infused us was pure love. At that moment, because we were sailing on a sea of love, we became that love; it changed our consciousness into pure love and the nature of love is to give and reciprocate. And in giving and reciprocating, we are expressing our highest selves.

> The goal of the spiritual traveler is to bring into full awareness their own latent spiritual capacity. Most often, this awareness operates deep below our daily stream of consciousness. Through focused intention and a course of guided training, this spiritual awareness can be released and come forward seemingly at will.
>
> Then daily, by making our focus and action the action of the Light, we reach higher and all the world benefits.

S.B.

*OK. Now let's get back to what else you learned in school.*

We also learned that all the religions were extensions of the Light. Across time, geography, and culture, religion varied because people were different, yet, on an inner level, united; it was this inner level or mystical experience that we drank from daily.

> While there are fixed points in each traveler's life; for the most part, life is something you make up as you go along. Moment by moment, the traveler creates their own consciousness, reality, and movement through the worlds. In each moment, there is opportunity for personal excellence. Always choose your higher self and you will never go wrong.

S.B.

*Why don't you give our readers an example of how this all applies in a practical example? What you've described is beautiful, but I'm sure a more "down to earth" scenario would really give everyone a clearer perspective.*

Sure. In the news there was a story about a famous athlete who had left his wife and was regularly 'visiting' a well known music performer; the athlete's wife filed for divorce and the athlete and music performer publicly stated their relationship is just a friendship.

Human nature wants to declare there is a right and wronged person, yet, we seem to be advocating, at least on one level, if this life is really all about us, it is OK for the athlete and music performer to be 'friends' and, in the process, conceivably destroy two other marriages. How can the "higher self" concept apply here? Do we have to abandon all previous notions of right and wrong?

*First of all, we may not have all the facts, but let us assume what has been reported is accurate, no matter how unlikely that is. Each person has*

45

*'free will,' and can do whatever they want; that is an underlying spiritual principle. Practically, it is very difficult to get another to do something they do not want to do, unless some method of force or coercion is applied.*

*Remember, some actions are better for us, in the sense that they bring us closer to the highest version of self; others take us further away. Each of us has an inner sense of what each situation requires and what is best for self and the higher good. In the past, this voice was called the voice of conscience. Now, in making our decision, which part of self do we follow? That part which is tied to individual desire and personal need, or that part which is connected to higher potential? For some of us a period of training or refinement is required so that we can learn to listen and hear that part of self which is tied to the highest. But we still have the choice that is the gift of free will.*

OK. OK. I understand that highest version of self and free will orientation, and that makes sense to me, but how about the traveler who says, look, what the athlete and performer are doing is simply wrong, a sin by our teachings; running around on their spouses and destroying a marriage, potentially hurting children involved? How does our spiritual philosophy fit this scenario?

*One could make the case that on one level wouldn't it be wrong to make either person stay in a marriage they no longer wish to be in? Or if parents do not want to be in a failing marriage, won't the spouse and children suffer or get a diminished version of their spouse/parent?*

*On one level, everything that happens on this plane of reality, the earth phase, that is, is neither bad nor good. It simply is, and depending upon your relation to the situation and the potential of the situation, serves a multitude of purposes. We cannot look into the future and know fully the outcome of events; what we are expected to do is use each moment, each experience, and each opportunity to reach higher for self and others. We need to listen to our inner voices, and truly hear which one is offering the best for the situation and an expression of the higher aspect of self.*

Wait a minute. Wait a minute. You mean there is more than one inner voice? Very complicated.

*Of course there is more than one voice! You know that; the soul has many layers, many experiences, which come forward in many different ways. Sometimes, in the form of a feeling, an inkling or hunch about something. Sometimes a dream or sometimes an inner knowing that this course of action is simply the right thing for you. Other times this knowing is a pain in your stomach that a thing is not right and to seek another course of action. This spiritual knowing, at times, is very complicated and other times, easy and very natural.*

*Basically, each traveler has to learn to still the many noises in their head so the inner awareness can come forward. That is the learning you had in the spiritual school, and where the themes of the present writing intersect. In the school, you learned to monitor all the different thoughts and feelings that were tied to the everyday life, so you could recognize the higher aspect within. Also, through the teacher's intervention, you were shown what the higher capacity could look like.*

So for spiritual travelers, the refinement of self that occurred in the spiritual school was to provide the learning and skills so that I could freely choose actions that served the higher destiny in daily situations. The point of this writing, for those travelers who may not have had this exact experience, is to inform travelers of the higher potential of every situation; that is, they too can learn to listen to that part of self which knows what is best. This is done through a process, and practice, of quieting everyday thoughts, through prayer, meditation, and contemplation to enable this inner knowing to step forward.

*OK. So, connected with this practical example, let's expand our discussion a bit and talk a little about the idea or teaching concerning 'sin.'*

*From the perspective of our teaching, outcomes or experiences are neither bad nor good. As we discussed, they simply are and clearly some are better for us than others. Some things in excess are clearly not in our best interest or health; too much of anything can cause problems physically, emotionally, and spiritually. But earlier we discussed that sometimes we learn something only by going through a difficult time; so what in the short run was difficult, or bad, in the long run turned out to be something useful, or good.*

*How about the traveler who finds their higher self only by going through years of addiction and self-destruction? At the moment, some experiences are painful, destructive, and life threatening; yet, the spiritual rebirth and joy, for this traveler, could only come about through this personal darkness. Darkness and Light are both aspects of the Divine.*

*The teaching of 'sin' is a fear based simplification of the higher teaching described above. On our spiritual journey, when we are just beginning, it is very helpful to have a clearly defined structure to organize actions and keep us away from experiences that do not optimize our highest potential. Also, this clearly defined structure is a useful yardstick to measure situational potentials against. To provide a simple example, we are taught not to hurt others. So, if I am going to punch someone in the face, I can measure my action against what I was taught to determine the potential outcome of the situation. It gets more complicated than that, of course, but you get the idea of how our early structure of morals and values helps us on the journey.*

*Now, let us go back to the situation of the athlete who allegedly strayed from his wife with a music performer. According to the teaching of adultery being a 'sin,' these actions did not serve anyone's higher purpose and probably were contrary to marriage vows/promises; yet, from the spiritual teaching of honor thyself and free will choice, one could make the case their actions served their personal needs, and in the short run clearly hurt others, but in the long run may be best for everyone involved.*

*So, who is right and wrong here? Remember, we have free will choice so we can make our own decisions, based upon the following criteria: that which brings us closer to the highest version of self. If the highest version of self, is what the self wants and needs at that precise moment, even if there is potential harm to self or family, then an action is taken with full awareness of potential consequences arising from that action. Also, from our perspective, there is a difference between what is harmful or painful and what a 'sin' is and where punishment can be expected from the Deity. All actions have consequences, and to the extent that they keep us from our highest version of self is our measure. If there is punishment from God, we are not able to speak to that point. Our view is simply that God's mercy exceeds His wrath, tenfold; and clearly some actions are better for us than others, and all actions have consequences.*

Each faculty of ours delights in that for which it was created: lust delights in accomplishing desire, anger in taking vengeance, the eyes in seeing beautiful objects, and the ear in hearing harmonious sounds. The highest function of the soul is the perception of truth.

Al-Ghazzali

## Sam Sayings

You don't solve one problem by creating another.

*

If you take one step toward God, God will take 10 steps toward you.

———————

Do not commit yourself to lengthy discussions of religion- such talk only succeeds in making religion a complex and confused matter. God has made religion easy and simple.

Muhammad

* *

*BRRRIIINNNGGG. BBBRRRIIINNNGGG. Time to wake up, and get back to writing. Wake up! Wake up!*

Oh, leave me alone. I'm still sleepy. How long have you been awake?

*Awake. That's kind of funny, because by your standards I never sleep, remember?*

Oh yeah. You are always awake; in your realm sleeping and wakefulness is the same thing. Right?

*Correct. Now are you ready to get back on the job or what?*

How about or what?

*Funny. Now, let's get down to it. What would you like to discuss next?*

Ummm... let me wake up here... Since we just finished talking about choosing the higher self and the concept of sin, how about discussing the very closely related concepts of expectation and reward? This again will help our fellow travelers put a more practical spin on spirituality, don't you think?

*Sure, why not? Since it's your idea, why don't you take the lead?*

OK but I need a few sips of my coffee to get started. Umm that's good; a caffeine jolt to the brain helps jump-start my battery. Just one more... Now, I'm ready.

Generally, people do things because they expect something in return. When it is in the form of a job, they perform certain duties in exchange for money that is then used to do many things. Now in ordinary life, while the transaction is not always as clear as monetary payment, in most cases, people do things either consciously or unconsciously, because they expect 'payment' of some sort. This payment may be in the form of 'good feelings' or the sense it is the right thing to do; rarely do we do anything without some sort of exchange going on; usually this is the way the world works. When payment is not forthcoming, as for example a hidden expectation of a 'thank you' or 'respect for our effort' is not met, feelings of resentment occur. This is the transaction mentality of ordinary life; many times people are unaware their expectation set is operating, but that doesn't mean it isn't functioning.

Here's another example from ordinary life within our culture: when someone holds open the door for the next person, the person holding the door open expects an acknowledgement of some type, and the person passing through has been taught this is the case. However, consider the situation where the person walking through is distracted, deep in thought, and forgets to thank the other for holding the door. Typically, a resentment or thought arises in the first person like, "What's that person's problem? Are they too good to acknowledge this simple kindness?" If they work together in the same office, the first person may think, you know, the others are right; he is stuck up and thinks he is better than others. Yet, the real situation is that the person was distracted by a problem at home; his mother is very ill.  But the transaction mentality has already gone to work.

*OK. Where are you going with all of this?  Somehow, you need to pull this together.*

Patience, my friend. We are discussing operation of the transaction mentality in ordinary life. Now, in both situations, either writing a book or holding the door open, something is expected; when it is not forthcoming, there is a potential for disappointment, hurt feelings and anger. All because the person has entered into a transaction state of mind: which may not be conscious, reciprocated, or entered into by others involved. Most often, travelers are not aware an exchange was implied. One of the tasks of the spiritual traveler is to monitor everyday thought patterns, so, in time the traveler can get beyond the transaction mentality.

When the spiritual traveler sees the transaction mentality operating, potentially, with a little practice, he can free himself from the effects. These being repetitive thoughts that are time consuming, possibly inaccurate, and potentially destructive. Consider how much time is wasted wondering why the person did not acknowledge the open door, or thoughts like, "everyone is right he/she is stuck up," or, "I'm not going to let them get away with that rudeness."

51

In this repeating thought cycle, blood pressure and stress levels rise, and personal energy is redirected from another use, and potentially blocks the higher consciousness from coming forward; all because the transaction mentality was operating and hidden expectations were not fulfilled.

> Along the path, expectation blocks your progress like a 10-foot high barb-wired fence. Always, travelers are expecting spiritual experience and special sensations. Each traveler must learn to recognize this obstacle, through peaceful surrender to their higher self and the higher destiny.

> S.B.

Now, one cannot minimize the effect of expectation, and how this plays into spiritual studies. For example, consider our underlying motivation, why do we want to engage in this activity of writing a book; is it to help self or others? Are we holding open the door to be nice to the boss so the boss will hold us in favor? None of these reasons are either good or bad. For the spiritual traveler, it is a matter of effect. Do certain thoughts, which are tied to hidden expectations, lead to other thoughts, which block the higher consciousness from operating? As you well know, the higher consciousness will not operate when there is a spike in emotion or excess of repeating thought patterns. The everyday consciousness must be relatively still, in order for the other consciousness to step forward. Sort of like, I was real still and sleeping and you woke me up.

*Touché.*

So, the job of the spiritual traveler is to free self from the effects of expectation, and do things because of the joy or love involved.

*Exactly, here is an earlier piece we wrote about this type of attitude.*

It matters not to the songbird
If other birds are there to hear its song.
The song and sweet melody
Arise from the heart and the notes must be sung.
The mountains, lakes, flowers, and streams
Sway to the bird's song;
They listen with an inner ear.

It is the same
With a traveler's life.
Each has a song to sing
And it matters not
If others are there
And hear the tune.
For it is the song of creation;
This song must be sung
And in the singing is the joy.

S.B.

Hey, I see a pattern here! We keep coming back to this idea of doing things with love and joy.

*You're catching on... and with recurring patterns in mind; here is a daily activity or technique to help our fellow spiritual travelers reach higher.*

## Daily Activity: Seek the Higher Road

*You know, most of us know what the right thing is; we are born with an inner sense of correct action and helping others. Religion prescribes service and giving activity because sometimes we forget to do the right thing or the business part of religion kicks in; a certain amount of money is needed to run the operation and we need to be reminded to give and help others. In your conversation and daily activity, 'try to help, not hurt;' as a guide, listen to your own inner voice, or conscience, which is a natural barometer. In the healthy personality, there is a balance between our own needs and the needs of others. In a troubling or conflict situation, if you are unsure what to do, ask yourself, 'what would Jesus do?' Often, this is a helpful technique to choose the higher road; and if this doesn't work and you cannot choose the higher road. Often, it is helpful to wait until you calm down and can choose the higher.*

*Usually, it is only when we are fearful, angry, or hurt that we seek to do harm. When possible, avoid action when you are feeling this way.*

## Sam Saying

In the ordinary personality, the mind is so constructed that it can only keep one thing in it at a time.

\*　　　\*

# 8

# Our Conversation Continues – Are You Really Saying We Can Co-Create Our Reality?

If you have fear, you have no need to think of punishment. Fear itself is punishment enough. Similarly with hope. Intense hope leads easily to fear that the hope may not be realized. To feel that one possesses something may at any moment lead to fear of deprivation. Feeling that one possesses nothing is a producer of fear. If you fear, or desire, beyond a certain point, you have lost your way, perhaps completely.

Idries Shah

Good morning, I'm back.

*Where have you been? We've been waiting.*

I had to have some fun, visit with people. You know, that sort of thing. This metaphysical, philosophical material has to be lived in the here and now. Life is much more than fine words, fancy sentiments and sending good wishes out into the universe.

*Aren't you in a fine mood this morning?*

Haven't had my second cup of coffee yet.

*Well, OK. Why don't you get your second cup and see if that helps. Before ending yesterday, what were we going to discuss?*

We were easing our way into travelers being co-creators with God, and what exactly all of that means. Here's a short vignette about searching for eyeglasses, that a fellow traveler experienced, which speaks to the point of creating one's own individual reality:

### Emotionally Charged

A traveler had just returned from shopping, been home for about an hour, and was now getting ready to go out again, and was running late. Before leaving the house, frantically she raced up and down the stairs, searching in different rooms, for her missing eyeglasses; earlier she had taken them off and could not remember where she put them down. Retracing her steps by making several phone calls to the stores where she had just been, she realized they were in the house somewhere. Again, up and down the stairs, getting more anxious because she was running even later; now, trying to decide if she needed to go to the pharmacy and buy a substitute pair from the generic eyeglass rack, until she could get to the optician later in the week. Certainly, her efforts were slowed by not having glasses on to see; usually, in past searches, she was able to overcome this temporary handicap.

All the while, her father was busy fixing dinner, observing this scene wondering where her glasses might be. This is a typical scenario in any home: where have I misplaced the car keys, phone numbers, or eyeglasses, etc. Patiently he waited for the situation to 'mature.' Usually, in a few minutes the object is recovered and all is again right with the world. This time, no such luck; so, her father calmly joined the scavenger hunt. Everyone knows it's much easier to find something when you are not emotionally charged and are actually wearing your own eyeglasses. In less than 2 minutes, her father found the missing item on a windowsill in the master bedroom. As he handed them over to his daughter, she asked where he found them; and remarked she had gone past the window several times, and did not notice them. Well, the day was saved and off she went, breathing a sigh of relief.

*Nice story, but for our readers, what's the spiritual angle or lesson here?*

Please give me a minute, will you? Talk about being impatient.

For those few minutes, her reality was supercharged by emotion; got to be some place, will be late, and I cannot see that well and need my glasses to drive. The process of retrieving the lost object was heightened by emotionality, which in part clouded "spiritual sight" or the ability to see. We all lose things and have a similar reaction, but the part that was individual and controllable, for the most part, was the level of anxiety and how we react to the lost item. In a sense, her reality for those moments was super charged by a pattern of frequently losing things and repeating this search and find scenario. There was good reason for this, not being able to see, and needing glasses to drive the car; however, her reality, or the way she under took the search, to a certain degree, was controllable and yet clouded by her growing anxiety.

*You're doing great, why don't you rest a minute? Let me continue while you finish your coffee.*

Thanks. I can use a moment to let the caffeine clear some of those pesky cobwebs from my head.

*For the spiritual traveler, reality is perceived and experienced. Through guided experience, the traveler understands reality is an onion with multiple layers, and at its center, seemingly, the onion is without* substance or form, yet, it is this 'invisible essence' that the traveler learns to seek in all things. This is the spiritual, inner core, which makes the onion an onion, and which the peeled away layers of our consciousness surround.

Each moment is here for a brief instant and then is gone. Within each moment there is opportunity. What are you going to do? Will you reach higher and embrace the highest part of self? When the teacher shines the Light upon the traveler's heart, the soul is alchemized from self-interest to a higher interest. In a caress of love, within the Light, the heart instantly realizes we are joined in Oneness. Within each moment, we have the opportunity to reach higher and join in kingship with the Light as co-creator. Inside everyone, there is an awareness of this potential.

In the spiritual school, the traveler is taught how to put on the glasses that will enable them to see the inner essence of things, and not get caught up, for the most part, in the frenzy of everyday living. In this way, both the Creator and creation may be perceived and known; it is precisely our emotions, certain ideas and thoughts, which keep us from seeing this inner connection. Various forms of consciousness while necessary and important to daily life, often block the hidden level from stepping forward. When we are super-charged with emotion or strong ingrained belief, the higher consciousness will not operate. That is why the traveler talks about stilling emotion and pushing aside certain thoughts and ideas. These thoughts, while necessary in everyday life, for the most part, limit capacity in the spiritual realm.

Perceiving the spiritual is nothing more than a trained extension of consciousness, and understanding some of the conditions necessary for this level of consciousness to operate. It is already inside us, operating at a level that for the most part is not perceived and used in everyday life. Getting in touch with this aspect of our being is a fundamental step towards co-creating our own reality.

To continue with the analogy of the lost glasses, it is like the person who is running around searching, needing glasses to see so she can find them. What the spiritual school teaches is how to put the "glasses" on to really see what is in front of you.

Say, has the caffeine worked yet? Perhaps you can offer other examples of how this is done.

Sure. Basically, the traveler is taught and shown that spiritual capacity is already inside and is the very energy of our lives. In our case, we met several times a week, for 4 years in Sam's office, during lunch or after work. Usually, there were 2-4 students present and we discussed a variety of work related topics, but quickly the lessons were directed toward spiritual learning. This was accomplished through standard teaching methods: question and answer; discussion of troubling events of the week, trying to understand the underlying mechanisms and our reactions to them; at different events, fellowship with other travelers outside the office; reading assignments of the classical and contemporary masters; and perception of individual spiritual states and our learning from our reaction. Because inner spiritual centers were being activated, spiritual states and experiences would occur anytime during the day or night. As a control, Sam requested that we report these and our reactions as they occurred.

Another way this spiritual learning was accomplished was through Sam's guidance as we meditated. After giving preliminary verbal instruction, on how to concentrate on the Holy Name, Sam *showed* us how to meditate and go deep within. Through transmission of spiritual grace, baraka, that passed through Sam we were assisted to concentrate and go deep within our self. It is this grace or universal energy that enables the teacher to do his job, and helps guide the student inward, past individual distraction. The universal energy gives us power, an "energy boost," so to speak, that allows the traveler to practice on their own and connect with their spiritual center.

Sam called this fundamental spiritual energy the Light because it dissipates spiritual darkness and is a palpable, living, creative force that the teacher uses to set the fire of Divine love aglow in the traveler's heart. This awareness, because it already exists within, albeit at a low level, can be enabled and activated from great distances, and, at other times, comes forward spontaneously exerting itself on the situation. As previously discussed, one of the most familiar of these states described in poetic literature is the oneness of creation experience; here the traveler is connected spiritually to all things and perceives their oneness in an ecstatic union of love, bliss, and spiritual energy. For those moments of spiritual awareness, there is no time or space only joy and connection with the beloved. Words really cannot fully convey the power of this experience, and for many travelers it is strong enough to initiate their journey and place them on the path.

*It seems we are going a little far a field here; let me pull this together by explaining more about the spiritual school and why it exists.*

*The point of the school and this type of learning is to help create spiritually completed people. Physically, the school may be located in an office, a bakery, a publishing house, a place of worship, a hospital or an international society to help disseminate cross cultural information. To the school, this is the outside form which has a viable worldly function and inside there is a spiritual mission. This training, experience, and guidance exist because the highest expression of life is to become a co-creator with the beloved. Spirituality must be in the everyday world; it is an enriching and enabling element. According to Sufi tradition, we are the King's representatives in this experience and in order to fulfill our function, must remember who we are; and in the process, regain certain forgotten spiritual capacities.*

*We are unique beings, and as such have both a singular and collective function. By using all of our capacities, physical, mental, emotional and spiritual, we strive toward human excellence and help make the world a better place. This is done through reaching for the highest possible expression of each moment. Inside all of us there is a 'divine spark' which tells us what the situation requires; this inner barometer or spiritual intuition when aligned with the higher destiny, knows which action will have the greatest benefit to all.*

*Now, let's return to the scenario of searching for our glasses. How might spiritual intuition or capacity have helped us? First of all it did; it was the energy behind the search. Fundamentally, we are spiritual beings having a human experience. What might have been useful for the traveler who was searching, was to remember an efficient search requires a balanced attitude; while anxiety is useful to get motivated and started, when anxiety reaches certain levels it can actually hinder outcomes.*

*Also, one can wonder, if prescience, or the ability to spiritually see things were used, wouldn't the whole searching scenario have been avoided? Yes, that would have been true; however, what the situation required was a calmer approach, not extraordinary capacity. You don't need a shot gun to kill a house fly, just a quiet approach, with rolled newspaper and a steady hand!*

*Here is another activity to help practice controlling your thoughts and daily consciousness.*

### Daily Activity: Practice Gratitude

*When you are feeling down, sad, or depressed, practice gratitude. When you are at your lowest, often it helpful to take a personal inventory and number those things for which you are grateful. Thank yourself or thank the universe for placing these things, people, or events into your life. Do this over and over; in using this repetitive cycle of replacement thought which recounts the good in your life; for those short moments, you will change your consciousness and the energy being created. For example, O Lord, thank you for this sunny morning and good, hot cup of coffee! Repeat this 3 or 4 times. Say these words slowly and with meaning; for those moments your energy will change and gradually you will get used to controlling your consciousness. Often, I find myself on a daily walk, thanking the Light for this joyful opportunity to move about in the sunshine. I repeat this over and over.*

*Remember, this more positive thought pattern has healthy and regenerative energy attached to it. And when you find yourself going back to your negative thoughts, don't get down on yourself; simply repeat more positive ones. Everyone has many things for which they can be grateful. Think about it.*

## Sam Story

Once there was a servant of God who was walking along a road and noticed a fruit seed lying in the dust. In the hope this seed would one day sprout into a fruit tree, he picked it up and tossed it into the grass beside the road.

In time, this seed matured into a large tree which gave rise to other trees. Over the years, a beautiful orchard lined the road. As travelers saw these trees, they stopped to rest and refresh themselves with the shade and fruit. Through the centuries, thousands benefited through this one act of kindness, performed by an anonymous traveler, long ago.

This forgotten act of kindness lifted the anonymous traveler into the circle of friends.

*         *

$-9-$

# Our Conversation Continues – Ancient Teachings Need a 21st Century Update!

> Everything is dependent upon remembering. One does not begin by learning, one starts by remembrance. The distance of eternal existence and the difficulties of life cause one to forget. It is for this reason God has commanded us: "Remember!'

Sheik Ismail Hakki

*If you don't mind, I'd like to continue and talk about a few things.*

Sure. Go right ahead; I'll just kick-back and listen to what you have to say. I'd like a little rest anyway.

*Now, in order to facilitate individual learning, the teaching is continually updated into a modern form. In this way, the spiritual or inner current is conveyed by a familiar cultural voice, and becomes easily accessible to the traveler. In ages past, religion, alchemy, and poetic literature were used. Today, in western culture, this perennial teaching has a scientific and self-help voice, and the teacher is skilled enough to teach in these cultural formats.*
*Usually in a variety of ways, the teacher presents the teaching to the student's consciousness. For example, the scientific framework speaks to one aspect of consciousness, analytical thought, while the spiritual or*

*inner current operates on a deeper level; sometimes the traveler is unaware of this multi-level activity, with much of the teaching taking place at night while the traveler is 'asleep.' This learning, like the ocean of life, is a series of ups and downs; like waves moving across the surface water, rarely is the surface calm and still. Yet far below, the ocean water is less turbulent. Here in the ocean's depth, the traveler swims in stillness and is suspended in a deep peaceful embrace. During this time, through the Mercy of the Path and the teacher's intervention, the higher soul is bathed in the Light of the universe.*

Excuse me. Excuse me. As you were speaking, I was getting bored and wondered, why should anyone care about this material? You know, it seems totally "out there," and it's not easy to see how any of this will help the traveler go to work every day and provide for their family. How about speaking to this point?

*Getting bored ... What? You want me to start singing and turn this into a musical?*

OK. I didn't know you could sing?

*I can't, but I can speak to this material's usefulness.*
*What we are discussing is the superhighway to God; the original human development system which is helping to create human excellence. We are offering a view into Sufi learning from within a spiritual school. This isn't jazzy or exciting enough for you?*

### Golden Path

Sam claimed that the path he was teaching was the golden path, the superhighway to God. It was the same path that had been passed down from the beginning and was the same path that Moses and Mohammed offered to humanity. This was the original religion, and mankind had distorted this religion into something else.

It was the fastest, most efficient way for the traveler to reach the beloved. All the other occult traditions and various sects were outgrowths of this primordial tradition. Sam claimed this method was perfected a millennia ago; there was no better system.

Sorry, did I hurt your feelings?

*Oh that was a joke of sorts, right? Not very funny!*

*And to continue, the reason why the average person should care about any of this material is pretty obvious. Right now, the world is a mess, and increasingly more people are searching for answers. We are realizing that government, corporations, big business, and religious institutions are not the answer to solving the world's problems. In fact, many of these institutions are causing these very problems; what is required is people who have a more holistic, integrated approach to life and realize their best self-interest is taking care of self and their neighbor. These more fully developed travelers go to work to do just that and by their actions become part of the solution.*

*We need to create people who are able to turn around the prevailing mentality of self-interest by stating, "I am my neighbor's keeper and it matters if someone is hungry and not receiving basic medical care." Better people make a better world, and use their energy to help make societal structures accountable for the greater good. This is only done through a spirituality that transcends personal interest and offers a methodology to incorporate the physical with the spiritual; this timeless system does this- and in our open age can be publicly offered to many people. Just as many people are required to solve the world's problems, so too, are the spiritual systems that guide them to look past the need for self-preservation and individual permanence. Being continually updated, this teaching changes to fit the given circumstances. On an inner level, people know the right thing to do; and need a creative spirituality that will free the self from personal interest and help accomplish the greater good.*

The teaching is continually updated and presented in a form the traveler will understand. This is accomplished by the grace of the path and living teachers; no community is without them. They are our greatest resource.

S.B.

How exactly does this form of spirituality accomplish this?

*Travelers who turn to that inner part of self, to help make their individual life decisions and create within each moment the highest possible version of self, automatically make the world a better place. They have no choice.*

And what about the traveler who doesn't go to a spiritual school or have this particular orientation, how do they make holistic spiritual decisions?

*Well, according to our tradition, there are two ways to accomplish this: the first being the natural way and the second, the unnatural way. The natural way is to follow Sufi teachings and this path. The unnatural way is to follow any one of the multitude of other systems with their random exercises and prescriptions. Potentially, both of these ways will get you to the point where you make holistic decisions, however, the natural way-submission to the Light, traditionally, accomplishes this journey in one lifetime.*

Oh my, what arrogance! Travelers who read this would think Sufis are arrogant know-it-alls, and full of themselves. How does this boasting qualify as spirituality?

*Is it boasting to say that penicillin cures infections? Or that Barry Bonds was the greatest home run hitter of all time? Or that water quenches thirst? These statements are merely descriptions of factual occurrences; it is the same with comparison of spiritual systems. This path is the religion before there was religion. Submission to the Light (or God) is the golden path, the superhighway to God. If you don't believe these statements test them out yourself; say the prayer of submission for 30 days, both morning and evening and see what happens. We offered this prayer in an earlier book and offer it again, because it is that important:*

> *O Lord, I surrender myself to you.*
> *I open myself to your will.*
> *Guide me through my life, and guide me through this day.*
> *Help make me into a better person who helps self and others.*

You know, we are asking the traveler to take our word that these experiences and the path we describe are accurate and true. Why would anyone believe any of this?

*First, we are not eliciting belief; we are describing something, sharing our experience of a series of potentials; a phenomena or learning structure, if you will. What the traveler does with this information or potential is up to them. Second, we don't expect travelers to believe anything, we are offering an opportunity or a way of looking at certain learning principals; we suggest the traveler test out these statements and seek their own verification; you know, individual verification is also possible in spiritual studies.*

It is?

*Yes, it is. Testing out a viewpoint or approach to truth and coming to your own conclusion, based upon first hand experience, is an important exercise. Third, any book written by an 'expert' on anything, essentially describes the so called expert's experience of something; the reader or traveler enters into the author's world, knowing this is only a written description, and it is not the actual phenomena or thing being described.*

*What we are trying to do, through this written structure, is create a measure of interest that will push travelers to seek their own answers. Hopefully, these words will reach the traveler's heart, stir the inner flame, and push the traveler to test out what we are saying.*

## All Creeds One

It is interesting to note that Sam rarely referred to servants of God as Sufis. He was the first person I ever heard use this term, servant of God, in referring to a holy man/woman. Also, Sam never used a specific holy book, and encouraged us to read all of the books. All he ever said was become a better Christian, Muslim or Jew. The servant of God points toward God. It doesn't matter what the specific creed; on a deep, spiritual level, all creeds are one.

\*

Krishnamurti stood up before a vast audience and in a memorable announcement dissolved the Order of the Star, rejected its world-wide organization and renounced the role so elaborately prepared for him over 20 years. "I desire those who seek to understand me,' he said, 'to be free; not to follow me, not to make out of me a cage which will become a religion, a sect. Truth is a pathless land, and you cannot approach it by any path whatsoever, by any religion, by any sect. That is my point of view and I adhere to that absolutely and unconditionally."

Jiddu Krishnamurti

What do you say we answer some questions about 'learning how to learn' and proximity of the spiritual master?

*Sure. Do you want to handle this or should I?*

I'm rested now. I'll take it.

One of the first things the average spiritual traveler gets into their mind is that they need a teacher; an expert. Someone who has traveled their path to completion and will also help the individual traveler make their own journey. A concurrent concern, along with finding a teacher, is which path to travel; there really are so many of them. Perhaps, the traveler will adopt the learning posture, a little of everything; I'll take a little Zen, a smidgeon of Sufism, and follow that up with a full course of Buddhism. Sort of like a buffet; I know what I like, already have everything inside of me, and will experiment until I find the right answers. All of the research indicates that all I have to do is remember that I have everything I require for the journey inside of me, right?

Well, that's only partly true. Let's keep two learning principles in mind. First, in serious study of any material, there is a period of preparation that involves learning simpler concepts, followed by increasingly more difficult ones. At the early stages of most learning, even the most complex of tasks does not require a master, but someone who knows enough to instill basic principles. When my brother Ben was learning his musical scales, he did not need a virtuoso to help him place his fingers on the piano or hear the variation in notes. There were many teachers who were available to provide this learning. Even before someone learns to be a surgeon there are many biology classes, frogs to be dissected, and memorization exercises. Along the way, many people are capable of assisting with the varying levels of skill learning.

Second, we don't always need a formal teacher to learn introductory or basic material; we can learn from all sorts of experiences, people, and books. Learning from a teacher is one method among many; with the right attitude almost anything can teach us something. In the beginning, much introductory material and many basic concepts can be self taught or learned from observing and reacting to the environment.

Consider all the things you first had to remember before driving your car; in the process of remembering the different items, like checking the tires, mirrors, and traffic flow, you forget to bend your head before entering and sitting down. Clunk. Now, you are seeing stars with a small knot on the top of your head. The next time, before entering the car, you won't forget to bend your head. In this scenario, it was the car that was the teacher and made the lasting impression.

To continue, in advanced spiritual learning that involves direct contact with the Infinite through a teacher, much preparation is required. It's akin to going to graduate school with multiple prerequisite introductory classes, assignments, and practicum. Not every student is prepared for this type of learning and, according to Idries Shah, needs to take time 'to learn how to learn.'

> All advanced or higher study involves extended preparation. Consider the work and preparation necessary prior to becoming an internist in a medical hospital. First, there is college; then medical school with multiple rotations and clinical practicum. With advanced spiritual learning, why do travelers think it will be any different?

> S.B.

This 'learning how to learn' involves using concepts like objectivity; or suspending every day thought and preconditioning to observe what is actually present and not what society has taught the traveler is present. Conditioning is essential and present in every sociological grouping, religious structure, and corporate and governmental administrative hierarchy. The simplest and most effective form of this conditioning is the fear and reward structure; if you do as we believe/say then you will be rewarded. Conversely, if you stray from our beliefs or disagree too much, bad things will happen. In a religious context, this proposal is presented, believe as we do and you go to heaven or in a corporate model: follow the company policy and you will be promoted, making more money.

The fear and reward structure is basic to the way we live, and serves many useful purposes. From the standpoint of the spiritual traveler, what is required is taking notice of when this is occurring, and, as required, temporarily suspending its effect, so one can observe what is actually present, then go beyond. Often travelers are filled with fear and not consciously aware of a manipulation; losing their capacity to objectively view a situation, and make their own best decision. The trained spiritual traveler brings to the situation a conscious maturity of sorts, and this maturity helps them to act in their own best interest and the best interest of the situation.

*Wow... well done. You're making me proud!*

Wait, I'm not done. There's still more to talk about here.

*Yes, we could go on and on and on! But how about the teacher's role? Whether he or she is in close proximity or far away, what does the teacher actually do?*

Teach. Was that a trick question?

*No. Be serious. Is it a lecture? Does the teacher give you books? Conduct question and answer sessions? Does it matter?*

OK. OK. It kind of doesn't matter, in a sense, as long as the teacher is able to connect with the student at the level necessary to advance the teaching. And that is strictly between the teacher and the student. What the teacher is able to show the traveler, in greater depth through various channels, is how their consciousness and thought patterns have been engineered by others, and connect the traveler with what lies beyond ordinary thought, the mystical experience. However, this capacity to suspend societal beliefs, because one is not overly dependent upon them, must already exist, on some basic level, within the traveler. What the teacher cannot do is give the student the capacity to be objective; it must already be present. However, with training and written material, the teacher can enhance this ability.

For example, most spiritual travelers would agree with the statement, all paths to the Infinite are holy and have something to offer. Also, people across time and culture are different, and that is why the Infinite is presented in many forms. Yet, some travelers find an irreconcilable obstacle in these two statements; because their path teaches their way is the only way, and if travelers do not follow their teaching, well, all sorts of bad things will happen. Now, is this simply a variation of the fear and reward structure or is their statement about singularity of their religious form factual? Is it possible for more than one thing to be true at the same time? Ultimately, that is for each traveler to decide; we are merely offering that authentic spiritual schools require a traveler who is flexible enough to view both sides of the argument, and experience what lies beyond this argument.

*Seems to me you are 'bashing' some of the major religious paths; why are you doing this?*

I'm not bashing anyone. I'm merely stating one of the entrance requirements for acceptance into a school. Within the context of finding a spiritual teacher, we are discussing one of the basic requirements, which is a flexibility of thought and objective evaluation. This requires an ability to suspend preconceived ideas and look at what is actually present, not what you have been taught is present. Remember, we are not telling the traveler what to believe, only that 'learning how to learn' requires the capacity to suspend belief.

*For spiritual travelers, another question frequently asked concerns recognizing a teacher, and how to know where to find one. Many times, travelers are drawn to a teacher because he/she looks a certain way, is well known and highly respected, has a strong media profile, or has said or written something which they found appealing. The following 2 pieces, offered by Idries Shah, puts a different spin on how to recognize real teachers and where to find them.*

### Recognizing A Guru

On a visit to India I seized the opportunity to talk to one or two spiritual teachers there. When I went to see one of them, a very important one, I was sitting with him when an American gentlemen who had made great sacrifices to come there, was announced.

72

He said to this guru as he is called, "Tell me what is a guru? How can I recognize a guru? Who is the greatest guru in the world?"

That is all he wanted to know. In that respect, this American gentleman's questions were very much paralleled by my own post-bag. I get the same sort of questions every day from correspondents who read my books. And this Hindu gentleman, who was the guru, smiled and said to the American gentleman: "What I am going to say will not please you. I hope you have not come here to be pleased."

And the American said: 'Oh no! I want the truth!'

'Very well, the answer is this. If I am walking through the jungle on a path and there is a stone in the path, and I trip and fall on the stone, and if I learn from that stone where I am going, that is my guru, because it has taught me something; not somebody who is going to teach me, not somebody who might teach you, but somebody who has taught you something. And if it is a stone, it is a stone. But you no doubt are thinking about human beings, about god-men.

'A guru is something or somebody from whom you have learnt something, not from whom you might or will or whom you respect or whom other people respect. If you can't learn, the teacher, effectively, "does not exist."

Idries Shah

### Signs of a Master

*According to the Risalat-i-Malamatiyya*, Bayazid was asked what would be the most important indication of a master who knew the secrets of the Sufi Way.

He answered:

"When he eats and drinks, buys and sells, and makes jokes with you, he whose heart is in the sacred domain- this is the greatest of signs of his being a Master."

Those people to whom you refer, who are devout, religious and absorbed, if they are incapable of detaching from these things- if, in fact these characteristics are obsessional- then they cannot be teachers of the Path.

This, in fact, is the chief difference between the indoctrinated person and the spiritual one, according to the Sufis.

It is indeed odd that this question still has to be asked today: over one thousand years after it was answered by Bayazid. This fact should make us realize how long it takes for knowledge to penetrate from being specifically targeted to being understood by people in general.

Idries Shah

*OK. Now that we have further "muddled the water" about what qualities to look for in a teacher; how about an exercise to help travelers learn, or be taught, from their daily experience. From a Sufi view, continual learning is viewed as a major indicator, in evaluating progress along the Path.*

OK. Why don't you take this, as I can see you have something specific in mind?

## Daily Activity: What Have I Learned?

*At the end of the day, take a hot relaxing shower to wash off the stains and stress. After drying down, go to your quiet place, taking with you a sheet of paper and pencil. If showering doesn't help you unwind, go for a leisurely 10 minute walk or listen to some peaceful music.*

*Before starting the written portion, sit and slowly take 2 or 3 deep breaths; focus on inhaling and exhaling. Then turn your conscious mind further inward; close your eyes and offer this intention: "O Lord (or O*

Higher Self), help me to remember and recall those experiences/events that occurred today where I might learn something about myself and others. Help me to remain calm and let learning lessons easily flow." Again, repeat your intention, slowly. Help remove any expectations that you might have about outcome by focusing on each word.

Keeping your eyes closed, gradually, experiences and events will be recalled and unfold before you: as if presented on a stage these events will appear- usually in the form of visual or emotional reactions to someone or something; or events may appear as an intuitive grasping of a situation; or recounting a pleasing or displeasing event. As you recall each event, indicate in writing:

- What happened? Use as few or as many words as you like to describe the event and your reaction.

- Write down what you learned from the event.

- Indicate why this event was important to you.

- Finally, write down how this event will help you react or try to react, in the future.

In the beginning, when you first try this activity, see if you can get 1 or 2 learning events to unfold; as you get better at recall, take the number up to 5. As this process of remembering and creating an intention to learn from everyday events becomes easier for you- this view of events will become part of your daily life. Practice this writing exercise for a month. Eventually, you won't have to write anything down, but you can continue to do so. You will be able to recognize learning experiences and patterns as they unfold.

In time as you recognize these events happening, whenever possible consciously enter into the situation and seek to reach higher by taking positive action.

If you are blocked, and this exercise is very difficult, get up and do something kind for another person. Make a phone call to a friend you have missed or offer to make a cup of tea for your spouse/roommate. Then add this experience to your list; indicating what you learned from being blocked, and what you learned from taking positive action for another.

*Remember, spiritual learning is intended to be a useful tool. Slowly, by sensitizing yourself to daily events and your reaction, this will help you take more opportunities to reach higher; and this multi-level activity will help you on the Path to spiritual learning.*

\*     \*

— 10 —

# Our Conversation Continues – Submission of Will, Freedom of Choice and Real-life Spiritual Experiences...

At every moment you choose yourself. But do you choose your self? Body and soul contain a thousand possibilities out of which you can build many I's. But in only one of them is there a congruence of the elector and the elected. Only one- which you will never find until you have excluded all those superficial and fleeting possibilities of being and doing with which you toy, out of curiosity or wonder or greed, and which hinder you from casting anchor in the experience of the mystery of life, and the consciousness of the talent entrusted to you which is your I.

Dag Hammarskjöld

*Let's further discuss the various voices in our head, why we must understand their operation and the shifting nature of consciousness. This will lead us to discuss the nature of the soul and spirit, and how this all comes together.*

OK. I guess you want to take this?

*You got it!*

*To reiterate, the basic format of this presentation is a stream of consciousness discussion between aspects of awareness. The part which is in standard letters is the everyday consciousness (the part we use to operate in the physical world) and the higher consciousness (intuition and spiritual capacity) in italics. According to Sufi tradition, with a little training, both streams can operate simultaneously, helping the traveler use their spiritual capacity in daily life.*

*Further, consciousness itself is a series of shifting patterns (Ornstein); some conceptual, some emotional, and others biological which are often intertwined, layer upon layer, and sometimes far below the surface; these layers emerge at different times and under specific situations; some are in the form of thoughts, feelings, urges or sensations like pain and pleasure.*

The spiritual traveler, on their journey within, quickly realizes that consciousness is an ever shifting and illusive thing. Peeling away the layers, like an onion and coming to find seemingly nothing at the core. Yet, this "nothingness" is the very energy of the spheres.

O spiritual traveler, perceive your own greatness; you are a being of Light.

S.B.

*Now on one level, while all of this seems fairly complex, on another level it is as simple as a deep breath of fresh air. The path has many turns, ups and downs, and goes on continually renewing itself in spiritual energy. From a Sufi perspective all that is required is for the traveler to love God (Light) with all their heart and soul; and to seek to make their life an extension of the Divine Will. For when one is truly in love, all the traveler thinks about and everything they do is for their beloved. This is enough to complete the journey.*

## Sam Saying

One moment's experience of the Truth is worth a thousand lifetimes of selfish prayer.

*

*All thought, physical awareness, and our very life energy, which helps create our body on a daily basis, emanates from the soul; the soul is comprised of a spiritual fabric and was created with a center or heart that is most like the Light. As the Light, or God, is greater than the creation, i.e., more complex, a part or aspect of this wondrous being is alive within. This is the part that will lead us through the many worlds back to our home. This journey may be accomplished in a moment, over and over, or across multiple lifetimes.*

*In fact, each time the traveler submits their will to the beloved, the journey is accomplished; this may be done in every daily activity or in a moment of sincere prayer. It is a matter of focus and intention; spiritual awareness is a natural part of us, which for the most part remains below the surface, out of our daily awareness; this is by design and at any moment can be transcended. All we need do is remember who we are; that is the point of the training in a spiritual school; remember who we are and in every moment, through love, choose the highest part of ourselves.*

*It is our higher destiny to use our spiritual capacity in daily life to enrich this experience. Each moment affords the spiritual traveler an opportunity to create their life; becoming co-creators with the Light, we continually choose what we wish to do and become. This is our free will choice; we can pick and choose among thousands of options. The traveler, who out of love aligns their will with the higher impulse, serves as God's vicegerent and according to Sufi tradition, does the work of the next realm in this one. For the next realm is purely of spirit.*

OK, so if I am following you correctly, what you're saying is that the traveler can both submit their will to the Beloved **and** also use their will to choose freely along this path of learning? Seems like the best of both worlds!

*Yes! That is the gift of this lifetime. Both actions are integral to true spiritual experience.*

*Now, each traveler enters the earth phase with a life plan, or overall destiny; and in order to accomplish this plan, brings with them specific skills. For the most part, in this experience travelers choose what they would like to accomplish; while the overall mix between what an individual chooses to do and what the guiding forces require, is both hidden and known, this earth experience is always freely chosen. On a deep inner level, souls are aware of what they must do, experience and accomplish. Much of life is totally up to us, however, on a higher level there are specific experiences to be had and learning that must be accomplished. Life is both fixed by destiny and up to us moment by moment. Both things operate simultaneously.*

Let's just take a moment to digest that reality. It's pretty intense. But then again, all of this has been a pretty intense experience, wouldn't you say?

*Yes, isn't it a wonderful thing, though?*

I guess... sometimes I feel like I am just along for the ride.

*I assure you, you are not! Now, let's get back on track. Within each soul there is the memory of all prior experience; this experience being in other worlds and previous lives. Remember, religion teaches: before we were born we were with God and after we die we shall return to God. This is the basic teaching and within this teaching there are variations, like the one indicated above.*

In the mystical school, we were taught and encouraged to test out and investigate all these sort of statements. In the course of our investigation, we would consult the spiritual literature; examine the writings of the great spiritual teachers, and listen to our own souls. Always, we were encouraged to leave our preconceived notions or what was previously taught behind, examine the evidence, and listen to our own inner voice that facilitates knowing. Further, we were taught that answers to these questions, while interesting, are not essential or fundamental to the journey; the journey was about loving God (the Light) and merging our will, at certain times, with the Light.

*Exactly. We encourage all fellow travelers to do the same, no matter what path they are following. Formal religion, spiritual teaching, spiritual experience, learning with a master, are all preparations for the traveler developing their own inner potential to know and make holistic decisions that are aligned with the Light. A traveler who is able to submit their will to the Light, as required, has matured and is able to travel independently. The teacher's job is to help those travelers who have the potential for spiritual maturity and independence, acquire the skills, experience and learning to do so. All travelers have an individual spiritual destiny, filled with wondrous experience and learning; some travelers are capable of more advanced study, and others, at this time, do not require it.*

*Consciousness is a series of shifting patterns, contrasting thoughts, inner voices, and experience. The spiritual traveler, through a period of learning, which includes examination of self, learns to travel through this maze and arrive at the center. This center is pure energy and Light; it is most like the Creator.*

So there really is more to me than meets the eye... a lot going on underneath this calm facade! I need to step away from all this for a while and really let it sink in.

## Sam Saying

When you come to me, come to me about God. Do not come here for anything else.

\*

### Servant of God

In our discussions, Sam referred to the saints and prophets of old as servants of God. As previously mentioned, this was the first time I heard this term, and it has taken me many years to begin to understand it.

The notion of a servant, someone who performs all actions for another, is a much easier concept to understand and embrace than the idea of a prophet or saint. These terms, prophet and saint, carry with them visions of holy men or women who somehow, in a magical way, mysteriously connect with God. Yet anyone can be a servant. We all have within us the capacity to do something for someone else in God's name. Each time we extend to help another and do it for God, instead of our self, we are fulfilling the mandate; and this is the ultimate purpose of our lives. For in this way, we draw closer and increase our knowledge of God.

\*        \*

*Good Morning! It's time to get up and get out of bed. How are you this morning?*

Grumpy and jumpy... that's how I am. What are you so cheerful about?

*Me, well it's time to go to work and start writing again. That's what I'm happy about and you... grumpy and jumpy. What exactly does that mean; sounds like 2 of the 7 dwarfs?*

You know, I don't like being awakened at the crack of dawn every morning, having to write down this material. On top of all that, you infuse me with this spiritual energy, raising our vibration to the point that I get headaches unless I comply and release it. For our readers, you must understand that unless I go along with all of this, the spiritual energy that is generated from my higher soul will give me painful headaches, unless I release it in this narrative. We have a story to tell, and fortunately for me this energy surge comes and goes; when we are in the creative cycle, it is with me for only part of the day. Over the years, we have worked together long enough for me to more or less understand the patterns involved, and know enough not to resist. In the past, when I tried to resist this energy, things got worse.

*Are you finished complaining? You really are a complainer you know.*

Yes, you have told me that before; one has to honor who they are. Isn't that sort of another mantra of the new age, self-help movement? "Be who you are."

*Enough stalling; let's get down to it. As you may notice, again, I am taking the lead on this, and our topic is spiritual experience; which in this dialogue and narrative, I represent. You are the everyday consciousness, and for the most part needed in daily affairs. When you are operating, I stay in the background and am more quiet; operating on a hidden or unconscious level, supplying the energy to run the body and consciousness. Yet, at other times, as you so aptly describe I step forward and exert myself on the situation; in the spiritual traveler, this level of awareness comes and goes: it is not a static condition. The earth phase is a multi-level experience, and the spiritual capacity, with a certain amount of training, can be called up like a program on your computer.*

Let me chime in here. Everyone has spiritual capacity and spiritual experiences. Just because you may not have learned how to recognize these things yet, doesn't mean you don't have them. We are spiritual beings who have taken on a physical form to express ourselves in this wonderful dimension.

*So now you are waking up and trying to be of help?*

Yes, so let me finish. Even before the training in the spiritual school, there were foretastes of spiritual awareness for me. As I

83

came to understand, these were energy "over runs" from the spirit which exerted themselves upon my everyday consciousness. In time, after the training in the spiritual school, I realized these experiences happened to teach me something.

Looking back, there were several instances of this, and I would like to share two of them. The point of sharing is so that travelers will look to their own experience and rethink the times similar events may have occurred in their lives.

The first time a window of awareness into another level of consciousness opened in my mind was in elementary school; I was no more than 7 years old. We were given a reading and writing assignment and, at the time, I was not a particularly good writer and didn't give much thought to writing. I think we read an article on coral reefs in *The Weekly Reader*, a national elementary school newspaper with informative pieces, and were to comment upon it. In my imagination, I remember myself swimming down far below the surface water in the ocean, scuba diving, and on the ocean bottom observing all the beautiful, multi-color coral, fishes and plants. In writing and sharing on paper, I was merely recording something I had seen and experienced; it was like I was actually there: below the surface, scuba diving and feeling the cool waters against my skin. I have never scuba dived, and it wasn't until years later that I snorkeled. The English teacher singled out this paper, I read it to the entire class, and I received an 'A;' this was the first 'A' I ever received in writing, and would not receive another for many years.

When I became older and began studying on the spiritual path, a couple of written passages helped put this experience into perspective. In one of his many books, Idries Shah indicated that the closest experience that one has to the mystical experience, is the artist's creative, holistic expression of reality. This intuitive, creative expression is accompanied by an energy or awareness that opens another window into the artist's mind.

Also, I recall Taylor Caldwell describing her experience of writing and describing the streets of ancient Rome. I believe she was discussing her book, Great Lion of God; a fictional, biographical account of the life of Saint Paul. Caldwell indicated that when she was writing, in her mind, she actually went to the places described in her novels; she was walking on the streets of ancient Rome, smelling all the fragrances in the market place, feeling the sun on her back, and writing from the vantage point of simply describing and recording what she experienced. This was the way she created, by living and becoming what she wrote about.

For those moments, I was scuba diving and going below the surface waters. Years later, I put on "different glasses" and learned to swim in the ocean of my spiritual awareness.

*Those were my first efforts at trying to come forward, you know – back in those days you pretty much ran the show!*

The second event I would like to relate, which served as a fore-taste to later spiritual experience, occurred during lunchtime while I was sitting on the hospital lawn, resting in the bright sunlight. At the time, I was in my early 20's and working at one of the New York State psychiatric hospitals; during lunch, I was watching the breeze and sunlight play with individual leaves of grass. As the grasses swayed in the wind, and danced in the bright noonday sunlight, for some unknown reason I found myself focusing on one blade's individual, varied motion. As I observed this blade, I realized each movement and angle taken by this blade in the wind was different; through the dimension of time, in the passage of infinitesimal moments, each swaying motion, no matter how many times the blade moved to and fro on the breeze, was individual and unique; while the blade might return to a particular position, through the added layer and dimension of time, this position had changed; but was connected to all the previous motions and any motions that might yet occur.

Seeing all the accumulated activity, together, before me in an actual design or mosaic that was simultaneously one and ever changing, somehow I felt my consciousness expand, shift, and unite with all the activity of all the grasses about me. Naturally and without fear, I felt myself connecting with and becoming one with an energy that supported this grass and the swaying activity; and as I became one with this energy, I became one with everything about me.

85

In that moment, which seemed to go on forever, I was connected through my own consciousness and the life supporting energy of the grasses to every living thing; it was all one and the same. And as I felt that part of myself expand and connect with this swaying motion and become alive; I was filled with great peace, joy, surrender and wonder.

Years later, I came to understand that this experience was a common experience on the mystical path. Because of the ecstasy involved, many travelers sought to repeat it over and over; yet the point of the experience, of course, was to teach me something. One of the lessons: reality has many levels.

*Are you finished with your walk down memory lane?*

Why the sarcasm? I thought we were discussing spiritual experience with the point being that every one has these experiences...

*That is correct. I was just wondering when we would turn the discussion to the experience of the spiritual school.*

I was working my way toward this; however, we have to keep in mind that not all travelers have the same experience and the experience they do have is all that they require. One traveler's experience is not better than another's; it is different and each is given what they need.

*Exactly how does recounting these two experiences help others realize that?*

Well, I had them before I ever thought of being in a mystical or spiritual school; they were parts of my life that were unusual, and according to all the teachers everyone has this type of experience and for whatever reason, does not look to the lesson or importance of them. Often, they are passed over and forgotten.

*What is the lesson or learning involved?*

Minimally, life is more than it appears. We are all spiritual beings with a multi-level destiny.

*OK. Now before we turn our attention to the experience of the spiritual school and how this relates to the traveler's journey, even if they do not have this experience, there has been something on your mind. I think we need to bring it out into the open," air it out" so to speak. I think it will help others.*

What exactly are you talking about?

*You know - expectations. We touched on it earlier, but its important here as well. And you know exactly why.*

Here we go again, bringing up what I expected to happen with the publishing of the first book and where all of this writing will eventually lead. Why do you keep harping on this? I'm trying to get past these feelings.

*Because it is a very important subject for spiritual travelers and people in general.*

How so? Why don't you discuss this for a while? You're the one with something to say.

*Touchy. Touchy. OK. I will. In everyday life, just about everything we/you do is done with an exchange or expectation frame of reference. If I work for an hour, I get paid a certain amount. If I love my children, it is expected that I will sacrifice and do things for them. These are some of the many assumptions, operating principles and ingrained behaviors of living in any society. We've been over this, but be patient as I hit some of the highlights again.*

*For most people, these expectations are automatic and travelers are not even aware they are operating. When expectations are not met, even when they are on an unconscious level, resentment, frustration and feelings of anger arise. This reaction is automatic, often intense and protects us from being taken advantage of by others.*

*Everything we do has expectations attached to it; even seemingly spiritual endeavors like writing a book to help others. Spiritual travelers are taught that strong emotions prevent the other thing from operating; in this dialog, I am playing the role of the other thing- higher consciousness. Resentment and disappointment, in daily life, when things do not work out as planned are normal occurrences. What the spiritual traveler is taught is that feelings must be honored, that is recognized, felt, and shared when appropriate, and pushed aside for a time so the other thing (spiritual capacity) can operate.*

*You are well aware that when you are frustrated about how people reacted to your first book or wondering why to write a second; the feelings attached to these thoughts, in the main, prevent me from coming forward, and must be 'stilled' for me to do so.*

Now, that you have totally embarrassed me, are we ready to drop this subject?

*Not yet. I wish to discuss expectation in terms of work and experience in a spiritual school. For you see, that when a student enters a spiritual school there are many expectations about outcome and the overall point of this learning. You remember how Eddie used to joke about becoming a saint and learning how to read people's minds? The point of bringing all of this up is that many people seek this type of learning for seemingly altruistic reasons that are covers for personal motives. This is normal and must be left behind. The traveler's need for personal outcome must be recognized and diffused before anything higher can occur. Also, there are others for whom this type of learning seeks them, and as they travel must beware of the expectation mentality. While these later travelers, for the most part, are free of this trait in the beginning, eventually and continually, expectation rears its head.*

*Personal expectation, both overt and hidden, is one of the main reasons travelers do not make any progress. This capacity to recognize, control and go beyond personal desire and emotional attachment is one of the key factors monitored by the teacher.*

## A Spiritual Teaching

Sam maintained that if we followed this teaching, we would become better Christians, Jews or Muslims. The point of the teaching was not to convert but to make better servants of God. This teaching was the inner teaching of all the religions and had been available to people long before there were formal religions. It was a spiritual teaching; not a worldly form that had to be incorporated into traditions and sayings. In every age, this teaching was transmitted in a way that could be understood by citizens of that town and country.

This teaching was the Light and substance of the world. It was the spark which gave life to the great religions and the prophets and saints were among some of the teachers. In fact, most of the teachers were hidden and carried on their duties in anonymity.

The great religions were all to be respected for they were manifestations of the Light. They were revealed at a given time and place for a specific population. Hence they were subject to the laws of decay, and what you saw for the most part was the shell of the original teaching. People focused on the form rather than the substance, yet, for some people this was enough. We were never to criticize another for their religious view. In time, as God wills they would experience the Truth.

Several times I can remember Sam referring to the fact that if this teaching was being presented in other countries there would be no question and answer. The teaching would be transmitted mind to mind, all on a spiritual level. Imagine a teaching without words. Can you believe it? At first, I couldn't.

At the end of some of our teaching sessions, we would close with a silent prayer. Sam would lead the session, and we would get a taste of the spiritual reality. He would direct the Light to each of us and we would experience it. This was one way we learned the real teaching was on another level. For us, because we were products of this culture, question and answer was important, yet the real teaching was something other than words and traditions.

Everything in the universe is comprised of a spiritual fabric. The infinite variation of this wondrous substance connects us all as children of the one.

*

The Sufis are those who have preferred God to everything, so that God has preferred them to everything.

Dhu-l-Nun

So, are you finished taking shots at me?

*Pretty much; what else do you think will interest travelers about your experience in the spiritual school?*

I think there are many things; let me take the lead on this for a while.

*I was hoping you would say that.*

Let me point out there were two different schools; first, was the individual and group experience with the teacher/master and then he passed us on to the next teacher; who we never physically met. It was a distant learning kind of thing. The point of both experiences was to help develop more complete people who were able to participate in the world. Spiritual learning was intended to be a nutrient to help facilitate and balance other capacities.

*          *

*OK. Where have you been? Nearly two weeks have gone by and you didn't show up to do your writing; you just got up and left without finishing the piece about the different schools. I think an explanation is required . . . Again, this might help the reader who is also on their own spiritual journey understand the ebb and flow of life, spiritual awareness, and the balance of things. I know we have gone over this before, however, sometimes repetition and multiple scenarios help facilitate the level of impact required for a specific learning to occur.*

All right; you know I am not one for the details of everyday living, but if you think this will help fellow travelers reach higher, here goes. Over the last two weeks, plenty of problems got in the way; there were issues with health, a car accident, work and financial matters to attend to. These things kept me from sitting down and continuing with our work. Besides the time involved, there was the necessary physical and mental energy to follow through, and the accompanying feelings of worry, fear, and stress. As you well know, life is a multi-level experience and the ordinary activity of daily living most often blocks the higher awareness from coming forward.

The object of Sufi teaching is to refine and integrate this spiritual awareness (you) into daily life; thereby enriching the life and enabling a higher, spiritually grounded balance to lead the traveler forward. Sufi experience occurs within the ordinary fabric of daily life. All of us did not come here to be saints, mystics, and gurus who live apart from the many enjoyable and challenging aspects of daily life. Even as we travel on the path, there is 'stuff' to do, problems to solve, dinners to cook, and loved ones to help. How's that?

*Not bad. Now let's turn our attention back to the spiritual school, what you learned, and what might benefit other travelers. As information for our readers, much of the Sam material first appeared in a self-published work entitled,* Servant of God, *which is an account written by two students (one of them being you) who studied with a 20th century holy man/Sufi master. What would you like to offer about the first school?*

You know, that is a very important question and presupposes that the traveler understands a few things about a Sufi school. First, the path, or the Sufi Way, is both individual and collective; there are experiences, which are specifically tailored for the individual traveler, and other experiences, which are for all students.

To over simplify and say, well, I learned this thing, for example, to *Love God with all my heart and soul,* may or may not be something the traveler who is reading this book needs at this precise moment.

For you see, this was the number one thing I learned, to Love God; for me this was the foundation upon which the journey was built. Yet, there are many travelers who may already know this or who are turned off by the notion of God. The word God has too many negative aspects connected to it, which are based upon early experience, for the traveler to learn within this framework.

For me, this was useful particularly when it was explained, that it was man who was responsible for much of the chaos and suffering on this planet. This was a choice, to hurt rather than help, which was being made each day by individual travelers. While many of the wars were fought in the name of religion or governmental sovereignty, in actuality most wars were fought about survival, trade routes, and land, power, greed and personal vendettas.

Each traveler has free will and moment-by-moment creates their own reality; God is all loving and intervenes when circumstances reach a certain level; many would argue the intervention, often, has been too late to prevent millions from suffering tremendous pain and death.

Yet, on another level, we were shown and experienced that there is only love. Through the teacher's intervention, we participated in this love; when the teacher reflected the Light upon our hearts, which is the primal spiritual energy of the universe our doubts were alchemized by this loving force.

You see, this energy, which we consciously became part of, was our home; it was all-loving, nurturing, and, while we could not understand many things, had our best interests in mind. To taste this essence is life altering; all questions and doubts are absorbed in this ocean of love; through daily meditation with the teacher, when our souls melted into this loving ocean, we no longer could deny that the very substance of the universe was this loving energy. We just knew it was the Truth.

While our minds could not understand why millions of innocents had to die in seemingly senseless wars, another part accepted that there was more going on here than we could possibly understand with our limited intellect and ordinary reasoning.

We were told that learning how to perceive this energy and use it in ordinary life was the religion before there was religion. This energy was the life force and part of this energy was already inside of us; that is why we recognized it immediately.

> A seeker went to ask a sage for guidance on the Sufi way.
> The sage counseled, "If you have never trodden the path of love, go away and fall in love; then come back and see us."

> Jami

In the first school, for me, it was through direct perception of the Truth that the learning began. On the day when I met Sam, all my questions about religion were answered; as indicated above, the teacher took the time to explain that most of the injustices of the world were choices made by individual travelers. Often these harmful choices were in the name of religion and personally motivated; all the great souls who have come here to uplift humanity, brought messages of love, peace, and caring for all.

In those instances, where prophets and teachers fought against others it was to correct injustice. For example, when Mohammed brought the message of surrender and fought against the desert tribes, it was to correct inhuman behavior. Current at the time, was the practice of female infanticide; treating women as sexual property; and general dishonesty and theft in the market place. According to my teacher, 'these men were for the most part, 'sons of bitches' and needed to be stopped.'

Now, while my mind was engaged in question and answer about God and religion, which went on for most of an hour, in that room something else was taking place. Gradually, I began to notice, there was an energy present that slowly tugged at another part of me; slowly, I began to feel at peace, joyous, and connected to every living thing. Smiling, the teacher offered that this state would stay with me for 24 hours and was God's present; it was an initiatory caress to lift me higher and teach me something.

*So, this information is at once practical and pretty "out there, don't you think?" What about the human ego and basic desires? How do you learn the proper balance? Is this something that was touched on in school?*

Yes. In fact, here's a story about how Sam taught us to deal with our egos.

### Moderation

One of the things Sam stressed was leading a balanced life. He maintained that moderation was one important element in healthy living and we should not deprive ourselves "in the quest for a spiritual life."

God placed needs and desires in us for food, clothing, love of music, and a safe home. It was just as wrong to deprive ourselves of something we needed, as it was to over indulge our needs.

"When the ego, or everyday consciousness, wanted something" (e.g., new car) Sam would say "throw the dog a bone." The ego was like a dog that had to be kept in check. It served a purpose and the task of the spiritual traveler was to learn to control and not destroy it.

Let's elaborate on the example of purchasing a new car. If you see a new car and really want it, what is wrong with purchasing it? Of course no one is advocating spending beyond your means or depriving your children of necessities in order to fulfill your wish. If you withhold purchasing the car and constantly desire it, you will never have room in your mind for God. By gratifying your desire, you are quieting the ego for a time and can concentrate on spiritual matters.

One time, I asked Sam why we needed the ego. I felt that my ego was getting in the way of spiritual progress. I was always wanting this and desiring that. I felt my ego was a hindrance.

Sam answered, "Without the ego, or worldly consciousness, we could not exist in this world. We would be tied to another mode of consciousness and be of no use in this life. The ego is a boundary between this world and the next. The task of the spiritual traveler is to quiet the ego and perceive the unseen world."

As time passed, I began to understand. We were created to serve God in this world. Part of our existence in this realm is to have a worldly consciousness and be part of life. We are to want things and then work for them. Getting a new car is fun, besides being useful. Also if we were not tied to this world, we could not be effective in it. The spiritual traveler must operate in both realms to be of use in this one.

Before we get back to discussing spiritual schools; a few words about spiritual states, their lasting importance and envy. As travelers, we were cautioned not to discuss spiritual states, such as the one described above with other travelers, family or friends; only with the teacher. Spiritual states are spiritual caresses; they last for a time, then, they are gone. They occur to teach us something. What is taught is specific to the traveler and appropriate to his current stage of spiritual development.

In listeners, often a discussion about these caresses creates envy and jealousy, as well as healthy skepticism. Unless the state is made public by the teacher, and then it is only for specific learning purposes; these are private and must be experienced and then left behind. Spiritual states are given in order to teach the individual traveler; these are not the goal. They are fleeting caresses, foretastes of higher consciousness; this higher consciousness exists to help others. Historically, many travelers confuse these states as actually being the ultimate goal of the mystical process, and for a time cease to learn.

Because the path is individual and collective, each traveler is given proof in forms they will understand. Spiritual states and individual stations (levels of understanding) are provided as necessary. In this form of learning, it is axiomatic, that if you do not know about a thing, it is probably because, at your present stage, you do not need to know it.

*Why don't you discuss what your teacher said about his teacher, and learning while asleep? This will help travelers understand something about spiritual schools and how ordinary distance is not an obstacle to learning. In the world of spirit, there is no time, space or distance.*

OK. Many things that the teacher said and did took a long time to sink in. In fact, he always suggested that we examine and test every statement and learning principle offered. We were given our natural skepticism and powers of observation and evaluation, as a protection so we might come to our own conclusion. The path was not a system of indoctrination, but a vehicle to learn about self and realize our own individual and unique potential.

Nowadays, many travelers are 'hung up' about finding a teacher; someone they can go to everyday or week and learn from. While this is an important aspect of this form of learning and many consider essential, consider the following information about non-traditional learning.

When I questioned my own teacher about his teacher, he thought for a moment, then provided me with an answer that took years to fully understand.

## Sam's Teacher

Sam said his spiritual teacher was Al-Julabi Al Hujwiri, an eleventh century servant of God who is buried in Lahore. After praying at Al-Hujwiri's tomb which is a famous shrine in his country, Sam was the given the authority to teach.

You have to understand my amazement and confusion at hearing all this. I was sitting with someone who communicated with dead people; someone who had been dead for over 900 years, and he told Sam what to do. On top of that, I was doing things that Sam told me to do. This guy talked with dead people and I listened to him. Now I ask you, who was the crazy person?

As time wore on, I put this account in perspective. Many people believe that although Jesus died thousands of years ago, he is still alive 'in spirit' and is able to talk with them in a spiritual way. In fact, many people claim that after 'praying for guidance,' Jesus answered their prayers, and on some internal level receive an answer.

So I asked myself, why did I find it so hard to accept the possibility of communication and guidance from an eleventh century servant of God? At the time, I guess my inability to accept all of this was due to my limited understanding about time and distance.

As the years wore on, I learned more about Al-Hujwiri and offer the following:

- He wrote the oldest Persian treatise on Sufism.

- His task was to make known facts about the Sufi organization and Sufi mission to the people of India.

- His titles are: 'The Selected' among the Sufis and the 'The Munificent One' among the people of India. He is considered among the greatest of Sufi saints.

- His tomb has been a place of pilgrimage and veneration for over 900 years.

So when we talk about distant learning and feel we have to be in the room with our teacher, in this form of learning, there are different standards and ways of looking at things.

\*

The Sufi is absent from himself and present with God.

Al-Hujwiri

Another unsettling way to look at learning is this second point Sam used to make, 'that the majority of the teaching occurred at night, when we were asleep.'

In our age, we are continuing with the exploration of sleep and what actually happens when we close our eyes for the evening. Where does our everyday consciousness go? All of us have had those strange jumbled dreams. What parts of our consciousness are operating and trying to tell us something?

In my own experience, I have had dreams that have come true; been in mysterious classes where beings of Light were reciting to me from books; and, after a short nap upon returning to normal consciousness, have been startled and frightened as my soul seemingly returned to my body, a fraction of a second late. My guess was that it was supposed to get there just before I awoke and missed the awakening moment.

All cultures have varying traditions about sleep. Some Native American cultures operate under the assumption that a person will have a dream that will foretell the entire course of their life and work toward this realization. Within the context of the spiritual learning, over time, I began to realize all sorts of things were possible. Where does our soul or consciousness go when we close our eyes for the evening? We need to stop thinking in a box, and realize that potentially, the entire universe is our classroom and playground.

## Daily Activity: Travel Inward

*Find a hobby or leisure activity that you enjoy where you can express your inner self. If it is working on a craft, reading uplifting material, gardening, going for a walk, listening to relaxing music, collecting coins, or taking yoga or exercise class, you want to learn to express the many, hidden parts. Each of us has a creative, spiritual potential, and in the beginning we must make time to explore and refine it. The creative expression of the artist or crafts men, where numerous factors come together; once experienced, will help expand your daily consciousness and help you begin to perceive what is possible.*

## Daily Activity: Repeating the Holy Name

*In some traditions, travelers are taught that by very slowly repeating the Holy Name (Yahweh, Jesus, Allah, Vishnu), with love and reverence over and over, throughout the day and their lives, they reach journey's end. Attached to the Name there is Light and energy; when you align with the highest, gradually, your energy becomes one with the highest. Throughout the day, try this simple technique of repeating the Name; see what happens. What do you have to lose?*

## Sam Saying

Just because you do not see a thing it does not mean it ceases to exist. The sun also shines in the night.

\*       \*

# Our Conversation Continues – Ordinary People Shining Extraordinary Light into the World

In cell and cloister, monastery and synagogue, one lies
In dread of hell; another dreams of paradise. But none
that know the divine secrets Have sown their hearts
with such like fantasies.

Khayyam

*I can see you are eagerly back at writing again today; sort of on a run
of sorts. Before we continue with learning in a spiritual school, do you
want to tell some of the readers about what is going on with you?*

No. Not really. You know by nature I am not that 'chatty;' more
of a strong, silent type.

*Yes. Yes. I know that about you. At the same time, it is one of your
strengths and weaknesses. But I think it is important that travelers realize
that a life that has added a measure of spiritual capacity, is still a regular
life; subject to all the ups and downs of living in any society.*

OK. OK. But you know just thinking about it is giving me a
headache.

*There you go again... using that old, tired, worn out excuse about a headache. Just tell them.*

Well, I am in the middle of a series of medical tests. My yearly physical turned up a problem in the blood and repeated tests have confirmed it. Now, I am waiting to see a specialist to determine what is next and understand how really problematic this might be. Is this a passing problem, or something that requires ongoing treatment? Meanwhile, I am being checked out by another physician, going through tests for a different long-standing medical condition. It seems much of my day is tied up going to the doctors, and as my mother used to say, 'don't let them get their hands on you... It never turns out good.' She hated doctors and hospitals, even though we had doctors in the family.

*And don't forget to tell them about your work problems.*

Must we go into that again? Alright, I seem to be one of those people with a "vocational maladjustment." Cannot seem to be happy with what I am doing; it's just the way I am. Always looking for something to complain about.

*OK. Now let us turn this to the positive. As your teacher used to say, life is like the surface water of a river, subject to waves that go up and down; yet far below the surface water there is a deep, calm peace. Into these waters, the traveler must learn to dive and swim every day; returning to the surface renewed and ready to travel.*

So, yes, I guess you could say my challenge over the last few weeks has been to keep on diving into my inner peace as often as necessary. Easy to say, not so easy to do. But the result of doing so is miraculous. Here's a short piece I wrote about Hope and Love that I'd like to share with our fellow travelers.

## Hope and Love

In this world, during any age or time, one of the most difficult things to offer another person is hope. Often the pressure and tasks of daily life beat people down and all they have to look forward to is a repetition of this circumstance.

For me, one of the greatest treasures I was ever given was the awakening of my spiritual nature. It was a miracle that happened to just an ordinary guy. With this came the realization that God loved me and had always been concerned. Evidence of this was Sam sitting in his office and answering my questions. It was as if Sam had some magical key which he used to unlock the door to my spiritual being.

I could feel my soul dancing and singing. Being set free into this material world, the soul was like a babe that came out singing. The spiritual caress lasted for a full day; it was as if I was walking in another dimension. I saw things for the first time and knew on a personal level that God was there and cared for me. God loved me enough to send His servant into my life to fill me with hope and love.

I cannot fully describe the enormity of this experience; for it truly changed my life. You see, if God cared for me and loved me; then God had always cared for His children. I was no different than all the others who lived before me or who would come after; this opportunity always existed.

Now to journey in earnest, I had the proof that I needed both on an intellectual and spiritual level. In our first meeting, Sam asked me all the questions about my doubts concerning religion and spirituality; and he supplied all the answers my intellectual mind needed. We spoke of the purpose and history of religion; God had always been one but it was man who used the difference in religious form to create divisions. This variation in form existed because people across time and culture were different; internally, on a spiritual level all the paths were one. All the answers were things that I had always felt or knew on some deep level. Sam had put words to my thoughts.

Also, through a spiritual caress, I was given proof on a deep, personal level; my soul was set free from its earthly chains and I felt for the first time my spiritual potential. I was a child of God. Who ever wanted anything more?

*OK. Are we ready to continue with our discussion?*

I guess so; what did you have in mind?

*How about we continue with the connection between individual spiritual learning and helping others?*

Seems good to me; do you want to take it or should I?

*Why don't you take the lead?*

As indicated, the outcome of this form of learning is a more complete traveler who is able to use their latent spirituality in everyday life. While each traveler is similar to others, they are also a 'one of kind' unique being. Hence, one can expect that the level and variation of spiritual capacity within each will be both similar and different than others. Further, each of us is born with a particular skill set, personality, and individual likes and dislikes; all of these factors interacting within ourselves and the world, as we try to live our life and give form to our own individual life plan.

Helping others is central to being a mature human being. Anyone who has been a parent or needed to help a frail and sick family member understands this dimension to life. Often, we reach our 'finest hour' when we are giving unselfishly to others out of love.

The goal of Sufi learning and personal development is natural: a traveler who is able to perceive, spiritually, the highest potential in a situation. This higher potential and the capacity to facilitate its coming into being are termed, work or service. In most travelers this capacity to perceive the higher comes and goes, and is dependent upon the situation. The spiritual master exists to serve many functions; one of which is unlocking and enabling the traveler's latent inner capacity to reach higher. In time, the traveler is able to help those around them do the same thing. This is all accomplished through the grace and love of the path; and the world is literally made a better place one person at a time.

### Service

**Traveler:**  Holy one, tell me of service.

**Master:**   As the stars in the heavens give light to the darkness,
As the sun gives warmth to the land,
As the rain quiets the flowers thirst,
So it is with all the creation.
Each is created to do God's work.

Be like the river that waters the countryside and gives to all the people.
Some will come to drink the water
And others will come to dump their waste.
Some will come to make their home
And others will come to learn the river's secret.
Like the river, let each take what he needs
And flow onward.

**Traveler:**  What is the nature of the service I must do?

**Master:** Each traveler is created with many talents
And the answer lies within.

Ask God, and God will guide you
To your destiny.

If you remember God's name;
God will fill you with strength and Light,
And your questions will have answers.

*Well, I guess it is time to talk a little bit more about spiritual energy and how the traveler learns to use it. Why don't you take this since it was you who had to learn to use it; and eventually, consciously link with me?*

All right, but since I took the last one, it seems that you are just sitting back doing as little as possible.

*Touchy. Need you forget that we are connected, and I am the juice or energy that is feeding this system? So how can you say I am sitting back, and taking it easy?*

I hate it when you are right. I'll just turn my attention to 'higher things.'

As previously indicated, each traveler is a multi-dimensional physical, emotional, mental and spiritual being with countless levels, within these areas, operating simultaneously. Consider our brain, scientists' claim we use less than 10% of the brain's capacity; one has to wonder what else is going on in the other 90%? Perhaps, one day our science will discover it was being used, but previously we did not have the instruments to detect and measure what was going on.

After the traveler has been in the presence of a teaching master, and participated in this form of learning, some of the limitations of modern science become clearer. Not all things are measurable and explainable by the scientific method or their instruments; consider the phenomenon of romantic love or the devotion of a mother for her child. How does one quantify or completely measure this with instruments, let alone replicate an experiment? Surely, there are some dimensions to love that we can measure: in the presence of our beloved increased heart rate; excitement and tingling in the skin; writing down romantic and loving thoughts in poems and songs. However, for the most part, the origin and flow of this beautiful dimension to life remains a mystery and illusive to the scientific investigator. Yet, there is energy and flow to love, as anyone who has been in love would attest.

According to Sufi tradition, there is no magic or mystery to miraculous occurrences that the Sufi helps enact; these events happen because of the working of natural laws that presently are not understood by most people, and that intuitively, if the situation requires, the Sufi works with.

This is spiritual science, and it is the birth right of humanity. It involves using spiritual forces such as Light and enabling potentials, through higher guidance, that are present in every situation. Even for the Sufi, exactly how all of this occurs is not completely known; it is a matter of intuitive capacity, and like love, defies complete explanation. Through the Light, the Sufi is able to use natural capacity that others may call miraculous. Surely, to us "everyday people," some or most of this may seem utterly unbelievable. Consider what I am about to tell you about Sam, and draw your own conclusions!

## Halo Effect

Besides being a trained physician who was adept at understanding human behavior, Sam had other skills that could only be termed extraordinary. At times, he appeared to understand the traveler better than the traveler him self. He was able to look into the future and predict events that would come true. Also, he was versed in all religions and understood every occult practice that I ever heard about. This instant access to knowledge, he claimed, was a combination of study and knowing; this knowing was through the Light and was given so he could complete his function.

I guess the thing that was most unusual about him, and something that we often joked about, was that there appeared to be an aura of Light or current of energy emanating from Sam. When we were sitting together and Sam was answering our questions, often we were stunned by the interplay of Light about him. Visually, there seemed to be a halo of Light engulfing him; which emanated and pulsated into an energy pattern, like heat columns rising from the summer pavement, filling the room with Light. This energy was loving, and wise; and when we were in its presence, we knew nothing could harm us.

Now, you may think that these experiences were limited to times when I was inside the office or in Sam's presence, but that's not the case. You never can tell when the Light will strike! Awareness is very important, even in your car...

## Electric Shock

Because I lived close to the hospital, sometimes, I would go home for lunch and visit with my wife and infant daughter. One day, before starting the car for my return trip to work, I decided to meditate.

With a new baby in the small apartment, often the car was the only place where I could get some peace and quiet. When I closed my eyes, focused inward and began saying the prayer (of submission), it was as if I put my hand into a live electric socket. I was shocked by some force that I can only characterize as electrical. It really hurt and stunned me. In fact, I did not want to try the prayer again for fear the same thing would happen. Until this point, the prayer had always been a source of comfort and joy with a gentle, calming peace attached to it.

Later that afternoon, when I saw Sam, he smiled and said, 'sometimes the teacher has to be careful how he directs the Light.' Sam brought up the subject, I hadn't.

Sam always said that as long as he was alive, no spiritual harm would ever befall any of the travelers. Also, as indicated earlier, he maintained that most of the teaching took place at night, when the traveler was asleep.

Putting these statements together, it appears that the teacher is able to communicate with the traveler, often on a level when the traveler is not aware. Also, that the teaching speaks to a part of the consciousness that is generally hidden. The fact that most of the teaching takes place at night when the traveler is 'asleep,' challenges many of the things we know about learning.

*Those are two great stories about your time in the first spiritual school. Besides historical reasons, entertainment or curiosity, why should any traveler care about your personal experience? How does it benefit travelers to hear about your encounters or learn that the Light is a living, vibrant and ever changing substance?*

You've got to be kidding. What happened in the spiritual school, travelers would want to know about this sort of thing, wouldn't they?

*Perhaps. To a certain degree, that might be true, however, the real importance is that presenting this kind of phenomena and material, potentially, will do several things:*

- *It will provide hope for travelers that there is a loving and all-knowing force in the universe; it is alive and well, waiting to be embraced through their own soul. Everyone makes a spiritual journey.*

- *Reading these encounters, if travelers become envious, may cause them to examine their feelings, prepare, and push further for their own experience.*

- *That the binding and creating force of the universe is all love and each traveler has free will to decide their level of relationship with this force.*

- *There is a spiritual force in the universe that is concerned about everyone and will help us all make the journey home. This force is independent of religion, and uses religion as one way to present itself.*

## <u>Daily Activity</u>: Prayer & Higher Intention in Our Day-to-Day

*As part of childhood, most of us have been taught specific prayers; some of these prayers become part of our lives and others we leave behind. Usually, specific prayers are different than praying. Prayer is a song that arises from your heart that you wish to share with God. This is a communication that springs from your very essence and cannot be taught; it is already part of you. Daily spend time talking with God; when you are doing the wash, walking the dog, or cleaning up the kitchen. On a deep inner level, there is a part that is most like God. Talk with and experience that part; that is our spiritual center and has traditionally been called 'the heart.'*

*Just about any activity may be done for your higher self and the higher destiny; when we are vacuuming the house, driving our children to school or commuting to work, by offering up this activity to the higher, the activity becomes something we no longer do for self, but to make the world a little better.*

*Try this offering-'O higher self, help me transport my children on time to the child care center, so, they will not be anxious about being late and enjoy their experience; and I will not worry about them. Help me with this activity.'*

*When you arise in the morning, who do you go to work for? Are you working solely for self or to help others and yourself? Are you picking up children at the sitters and raising them to be more complete people, or better consumers of all the things they want? Begin to consider your motivation and intention, so, you can turn it over as a prayer to the higher, and everyone can travel further.*

You did not exist when your work was created: You were created from a sea of work.

Shabistari

*

The first step is to say, 'God,' and nothing else; the second is intimacy; and the third is to burn.

Attar

*     *

— 12 —

## Our Conversation Continues – Proof, Miracles, Belief, and Moving On from the First School

The massive institutional religion, according to the Sufis, also undergoes experiences which produce, first, the fossil stage, where people have to be conditioned to believe since it can no longer supply the inner experience which is now locked within its teaching or sacraments. After this comes the period of disillusionment: which in turn leads to the post-liturgical stage; when the stream of truth can again intervene: starting the cycle once more.

Chawan Thurlnas

So, do you think it is OK to keep giving examples of our encounters in the spiritual school? Won't these stories make travelers jealous or be written off as remembrances of a deluded person? After all, ironically, they were in a psychiatric hospital, and everyone knows only crazy people go to work in these places.

*Look, that is one of the themes of this book, and people will make whatever they want out of this. Yes. Recounting these experiences might create envy or be written off as well intentioned but exaggerated; particularly, that material about the Light. Skeptics will say, poor fellow, he was just hypnotized or talked himself into believing it. Yet, others will think*

111

*objectively about what we are reporting and begin to wonder. Perhaps, some travelers might even wish to find their own experience and answers. Our job in all of this is to present the material, and let other factors go to work. This is a more open time, and many travelers want to know; many are seeking personal experience and answers.*

OK. At this point, let's talk about miracles and personal proof. Before offering the following two stories, let me stress that from a Sufi perspective, miracles are the operation of natural, spiritual laws that are simply not understood by most travelers.

### Miracle #1

What are miracles and do they actually occur? Most people when pressured might respond that a miracle is an extraordinary event that goes beyond the natural laws. It is something special and rarely happens; usually, performed by someone who looks like Moses in the movie 'The Ten Commandments.' I'm sure that most people want to believe in miracles, but really don't. They have a natural doubt and skepticism, which is healthy. I guess I was no different than anyone else, until I met Sam and he changed my life. Then I began to look at miracles almost as if they were commonplace.

Sam was the type of individual who could look at you and somehow know everything about you. He could look into your soul and tell you things about yourself that you didn't know; also, he could tell you things that were about to happen: and they would happen. He was uncanny and according to his own estimate, was correct 90% of the time.

To me, it was a miracle that Sam intervened in my life. I never thought about God, or put a name to the emptiness inside. It was only by sitting with Sam and experiencing the Light that he somehow reflected, that I knew that God existed. Being with Sam made me know there was a God, not just believe it. I had proof on a personal spiritual level that there was a unifying reality that governed the universe. I had this proof by sitting beside one of God's representatives. The miracle of faith and knowledge was somehow turned on by being in that man's presence. It was if Sam had the key and unlocked the door. Then I became aware of a part of me that had been asleep.

On an intellectual level, I accepted that everyone had a spiritual nature, but I had never really consistently experienced that part of myself, until the day I met Sam. The experiences described earlier, about writing and movement of grass, were like momentary flickers of a candle. Awakening and refining my spiritual nature was the outcome that accompanied my time with Sam. I knew this time was special and out of the ordinary. Because what he did had never happened to me before. So to me, the spiritual journey has always been a journey that started with a miracle: a miracle of faith.

### Miracle #2

There is a second story, which was another miracle of sorts. When my wife and I were trying to conceive our first child, we were having a very difficult time. Neither my wife nor I realized, because the doctors kept it from us, that my wife had a sickly ovary and they doubted whether we could have children at all. Finally, our doctor prescribed fertility pills for my wife, because nothing was working. At the time, medically this was the most extreme and aggressive treatment available. I can remember that the pills were not covered by our medical plan and very expensive. We were also nervous about the multiple births that often accompanied their use.

When I explained our difficulties to Sam, who was a physician, he told us to try something else before using the fertility pills. He reasoned, why not try his advice, we could always wait a little bit longer to try the pills.

So, that evening my wife and I showered and before joining, we asked God for guidance and help in having a baby. That evening, as we slept, my wife and I both had dreams. Separately, we were both told that a baby girl was conceived that night.

In her dream, my wife was visited by her deceased mother, who helped pick out the colors and furniture for her granddaughter's room. In my dream, I was visited by angels, who sang that from a sickly womb a baby girl was born of whom the angels would sing praises.

Months later after my wife delivered, we were told by the two doctors who treated our female family members for over 25 years, they never thought she could conceive. We never used the fertility pills, and in the birthing process, somehow, my wife's sickly ovary has healed. We were able to have a second child without a problem. The doctors themselves called it a miracle birth. We never told them about Sam's instructions or the dreams. The doctors were the first to use the word miracle, not us.

Also, when we shared the good news with Sam, coupled with the description of the two dreams, Sam replied, "and some people believe there was only one virgin birth." To this day, I'm not sure what that statement means; obvious meanings arise, but the exact nature of it all is very illusive, and challenges many cherished beliefs.

Now, in examining the criteria for a miracle- something out of the ordinary performed by someone looking like a Hollywood portrayal of Moses- the only part that was missing was the long beard and flowing robes. We were able to have a child, where it was believed that none could be conceived. This was due to the intervention of another person in an extraordinary fashion. Sam used some spiritual science or inspiration to prescribe the correct antidote, and as God willed, a baby girl was born.

*

There can be no greater foolishness than to deny the reality of something only because one has not experienced it.

Al Ghazzali

*

In the journey, each traveler is both question and answer. No traveler believes without denying and knows without direct experience.

S.B.

*

So far, we've talked a lot about the first mystical school and some of our experiences. Also, we tried to connect up those experiences both with our daily life and the impact of spiritual learning. What's next? You're the overall guiding aspect to this work, so, what direction do you think we need to take?

*Hold on a second. Let's not forget that you and I are connected and it's not just up to me; you have a say in all of this you know. What direction do you think we should take?*

Well, I've been stumped for a direction and reaching for something . . . On this, I thought you could bail us out?

*Come on, push harder. . . you can get it.*

All right! You're not letting me off the hook; are you?

*No. I'm not.*

We still have not discussed the second school nor how throughout my life, this learning matured, becoming a regular part of my day.

*Well. I think if we talk about the second school, we can get into the long-term effects of this learning. Remember, how you worked part-time on your doctoral dissertation for nearly 9 years? In part, that prepared you for the second phase of spiritual learning.*

How so?

*Well, suppose someone told you; look I have this job for you. It's real important and it will take you 9 years or so to complete it. Now, most travelers would hesitate at beginning something like this; not sure if they wish to invest the time or could work on something for that long. However, while working on your dissertation, you learned how to pace yourself and how to deal with disappointment; even giving up several times, but later giving yourself permission to start up again, until you finished. Well, studying and working on anything across a lifetime is much like this. There are many ups and downs. Get it?*

Sure. Sort of like what we do with our lives. Without realizing it, we work on many things across a lifetime. We came here to experience, work and love, serve, and co-create.

*You got it. So when someone sends you a letter and indicates if you really are serious about studying this material, totally familiarize yourself with these 20 books; then write for more instructions, you wouldn't blink? Right?*

That was a low blow. Do we have to go into all of that as well?

*Yes. Now, let's begin telling the story of the second school, OK?*

OK. As much as it embarrasses me to share this with all of you, here it goes...

## Kicking us out of the Nest

One day, after about nearly 4 years, Sam called us (Zach, Eddie and myself) into his office, and said, this phase of learning was over. Now, it was time to pass us on to the next teacher. Each of us was to write the Society for Sufi Studies, P.O. Box 43, Los Altos, CA 94022 and wait for instructions.

Leaving Sam's office that day, we were all shocked and unsure what these instructions meant. Over time, this action became clearer, and can be likened to studying in one school, acquiring the skills necessary to graduate; then moving on to the next level of training. The difference is with most schools you know when the time has come to move on; the teacher doesn't have to tell you.

Sam kicked the young birds out of the nest to see if they could fly on their own. This is a traditional technique, where students spend time with one teacher, and then after a period of preparation, at the teacher's instruction, move onto the next teacher. In each experience, the traveler learns different aspects about self and the path.

Since we all worked at the same hospital, Sam was gracious whenever he saw us, and on several occasions invited us to his office for coffee; however, while the coffee and the love and kindness were the same, the conversation shifted. Now, it was purely social: about people at work, and the health of family members. No longer were questions about the spiritual journey answered; whenever these were raised by one of us, Sam shifted the conversation. Quickly we realized, the wonderful days of drinking in the Light at the teacher's side were over. Now, it was time to test our learning and expand our understanding of spiritual studies.

Like the others, I wrote the Society for Sufi Studies and after 6 months received a reply. This letter was from the Organizational Director, who acknowledged my interest and indicated that if still interested and I wished to continue with Sufi Studies, I needed to read the following 20 books written by Idries Shah; a list was included. Then, when I had totally familiarized myself with their contents, I was to write again for further instruction.

While the letter and instructions were very clear, I was confused. I had already read 5 books by Shah, and, at Sam's direction, been studying this Sufi material, now, for about 4 (+) years. Also, I felt this letter was a little insulting and had not acknowledged my efforts to date. So, I wrote the Director and indicated the above objections; further stating, that I simply did not have the money to purchase all 20 of the books, and was 'put off' by the whole thing.

A few days later, when I met Sam at work and related this story, he said nothing, but looked so very embarrassed by my action, that I immediately realized I had made a serious mistake. After work that night, I again wrote the Director, apologized for my 'poison pen letter,' and indicated that I would set about the task. Fortunately for me, that 'stinging' first reply letter was never formally acknowledged or answered. Sometimes, no answer is an answer.

Nowadays, with the Internet and so many schools and colleges offering long distance degrees, the concept of learning at a distance is more familiar. However, consider a spiritual school that at a distance is able to assist learners all across the world by offering a body of written material and monitoring outcomes; sending energy to its learners while they are sleeping; and helping provide for the traveler during their daily life, all the practical experience necessary.

For the spiritual traveler, the following information is offered concerning this form of learning; some of which was told to me, some of which is public information and other aspects, over time, I either learned or pieced together.

- *Spiritual Enrollment.* Sam indicated that at the point of writing our initial letter to the Society for Sufi Studies, we were enrolled; the period of waiting, six months, for our instructions was used to discourage those students who were not serious.

- *Teacher of the Age.* Idries Shah, who founded the Society for Sufi Studies, died in 1996 and was universally considered to be the Sufi Teacher of the Age. This is no insignificant designation, and while this title may be unfamiliar to most westerners, traditionally it is very rarely used and indicates a supremely gifted individual. Shah's body of written material for the spiritual traveler supersedes all previous written Sufi material; contained in those 20 books which are the required reading, is everything in written form the western traveler needs for their journey. For his later responsibilities, Shah was groomed and educated at a very early age, and this body of material was compiled specifically for our time; in order to help create spiritually developed travelers, who, God willing participate in the world and may help save us from ourselves.

- *Study the Material.* Well, I believe it took me well over 10 years to totally familiarize myself with the titles and their material, as indicated in the original letter. After studying this material, all my spiritual questions were answered, and there was no need to further contact the Society with questions. The content of the books, the many stories and jokes tell you what to do; you see there is a whole body of material that is the birthright of humanity and has been collected specifically by Shah and others to help make better travelers, one person at a time. Also, there were different materials (books, CD/DVD) that were offered by the Society that are both interdisciplinary and cross-cultural and helped expand my way of looking at things. Most of this written material and audio/visual products are offered at discounted prices; with the intention of making it all easily available.

- *Learning On Many Levels.* Traditionally, the world is viewed as a giant market place and classroom; when the right factors combine, we all can get whatever we need. While my mind was busy reading the books and listening to the tapes, there was another part of me, that on a deep, inner level was busy absorbing and drinking it all in; and, at certain times, helped me see the direct application in my daily life. For example, Shah presents 1500 or so Middle Eastern teaching stories, which are traditional and help the traveler unlock the hidden motivations of everyday activity. These stories, in part, are offered as snapshots of human behavior, and for the reader, work on an unconscious level, so, when we see a parallel of this story in everyday life, we know to expect certain outcomes.

- *Direction from a Distance.* Slowly, what I came to realize was just like a traditional distance learning college, in this spiritual school, the progress of individual students was monitored. While in more familiar learning environments, this comes in the form of tests, papers, and assignments: for the spiritual traveler, life is the great classroom and we test out, daily, the specific learning. Also, when we are asleep and our daily consciousness is resting, other types of learning impacts occur: in my own case, I can remember being read passages from books, the activation of individual spiritual centers, and parts of my consciousness talking to other parts. This dialogue between aspects of consciousness was much like what is being represented here. For the skeptic, and you should be skeptical, let's put this in a different frame of reference. As previously discussed, many people believe that their prayers are answered by Jesus who died well over 2000 years ago. So, why is it so hard to accept, that within another spiritual framework, contact occurs on levels that are not completely understood or reported in our western culture on a daily basis?

- *A Plan for Humanity.* According to Sufi tradition, there is a plan for humanity, and the hidden friends are guardians of this plan. Humanity is evolving upward and must freely choose the higher destiny, one person at a time. The hidden friends correct deviations in this plan and daily project the Light into this physical world. This Light is the life giving force and without its presence we would wither and die.

Now, as improbable as this may sound, particularly, as we gaze about and consider all the cruelty, greed, and problems of our current world, for the Sufi, this spiritual presence with its assurances is an ever-present reality. Having embraced the Light, been placed on the path by a living master, and experienced my own spiritual nature, all of this is second nature; because the spiritual traveler has lived it, and realizes that without this guiding presence, the world would be much worse off and become even darker. Spiritually, just as personal interventions can occur, then it is so for all travelers. If the traveler, would like more information about this tradition of hidden guidance see, Ernest Scott, People of the Secret, Octagon Press, London, 1983.

## Daily Activity: Relaxing, Cleansing

*Because we are multi-level beings, we must maintain a balance, or healthy level of homeostasis, so we can access what lies deep within. When we are in physical or emotional pain, it is very difficult to travel inward. Also, when our muscles are tense and we are experiencing troubling, repeating thoughts, the journey inward is further slowed. That is why often the prescription to make the daily, inner journey is begun with a cleansing of sorts. As a form of readiness, a hot, relaxing shower to clean-off the 'dirt' of the day, or a deep breathing exercise to connect with our inner rhythm and bring refreshing air and oxygen into our system is often suggested. Relaxing, cleansing activity helps tune and make us ready to connect with our inner current.*

## Sam Sayings

One moment's experience of the Truth is worth a thousand lifetimes of selfish prayer.

\*

When you are feeling depressed get up and do something for someone else.

\*        \*

# — 13 —

# Our Conversation Continues – Everyday Spirituality

If you could get rid of yourself just once, the secret of secrets would open to you. The face of the unknown, hidden beyond the universe would appear on the mirror of your perception.

Rumi

Now, that we have filled the spiritual traveler's head with all of this, which for some will sound like it is right out of a science fiction movie, where are we going with this?

*Oh, you who have little faith. What makes you think that travelers cannot benefit from putting this information out there? We don't expect travelers to accept these statements 'as gospel,' but to examine them like any hypothesis and test them out. What we hope is that these statements are not rejected totally, but investigated, and on some level looked at as potentially true, until proven or supported by personal experience.*

*Also on some level, it is reassuring that this crazy planet is being looked after, and perhaps humanity will not destroy itself, because individuals will reach higher, with the assistance of the hidden friends, and do the right thing.*

OK. That makes sense; just because I accept something, doesn't mean others need to accept it. The universe is an awfully big place, and all kinds of things are possible. By the way, for the spiritual traveler who is unaware of our traditions, who are these hidden friends, anyway?

*In order to enact the plan and fulfill their function as guardians, numbers of servants with different jobs are required; being a teacher is just one role. Most of these servants are hidden; this is by design, because these servants have work to do, and don't have time to explain what they are doing. Like a surgeon performing an operation, there is no time for questioning, only directed action to help the patient. Within this administrative hierarchy, like a large corporation, spiritual duties are delegated at various levels and for the most part are mysterious and unknown; the spiritual traveler does not need to know about these roles to get their job done - which is to add personal spiritual capacity.*

*A well-known story from the Koran, of our inability to understand the mysterious workings of the spiritual realm, is contained in the story of Moses and Khidr. In this story, Moses requests to accompany Khidr, the hidden guide of the Sufis who travels the earth intervening anonymously in affairs, to learn about higher knowledge and promises not to inquire or interfere, when Khidr intervenes in events.*

### Moses and Khidr

Moses said to him: Shall I follow you on condition that you should teach me right knowledge of what you have been taught?

Khidr said: Surely you cannot have patience with me.

And how can you have patience in that of which you have not got a comprehensive knowledge?

Moses said: If Allah pleases, you will find me patient and I shall not disobey you in any matter.

124

Khidr said: If you would follow me, then do not question me about any thing until I myself speak to you about it.

So they went their way until when they embarked in the boat Khidr made a hole in it. Moses said: Have you made a hole in it to drown its inmates? Certainly you have done a grievous thing.

Khidr said: Did I not say that you will not be able to have patience with me?

Moses said: Blame me not for what I have forgot and do not constrain me to a difficult thing in my affair.

So they went on until, when they met a boy, Khidr slew him. Moses said: Have you slain an innocent person otherwise than for manslaughter? Certainly you have done an evil thing.

Khidr said: Did I not say to you that you will not be able to have patience with me?

Moses said: If I ask you about anything after this, keep me not in your company; indeed you shall have then found an excuse in my case.

So then they went on until when they came to the people of a town, they asked them for food, but they refused to entertain them as guests. Then they found a wall which was on the point of falling, so Khidr put it into a right state. Moses said: If you had pleased, you might certainly have taken a recompense for it.

Khidr said: This shall be the separation between me and you; now I will inform you of the significance of that with which you could not have patience.

As for the boat, it belonged to some poor men who worked on the river and I wished that I should damage it, and there was behind them a king who seized every boat by force.

And as for the boy, his parents were believers and we feared lest he should make disobedience and ingratitude to come upon them:

So we desired that their Lord give them in his place one better than him in purity and nearer to having compassion.

And as for the wall, it belonged to two orphan boys in the city, and there was beneath it a treasure belonging to them, and their father was a righteous man; so your Lord desired that they should attain their maturity and take out their treasure, a mercy from your Lord, and I did not do it on my own accord. This is the significance of that with which you could not have patience.

Koran, Sura 18: 66-82

That's a great story about the mysterious workings of the larger, spiritual realm; but let's take the discussion to an individual level. How does the average spiritual traveler add personal spiritual capacity?

*According to St. John of the Cross, the process of spiritual enlightenment comes from two directions- externally and internally- and may be compared to a moist log that is thrown onto the fire to burn. In order to fully burst into flames, the log must be externally and internally heated; as the outside moisture on the log slowly dries up, from the heat of the flames, also the log dries internally as the internal temperature rises, then suddenly the log bursts aflame from inside and out.*

*In this analogy, the external heat, is the activity of the everyday consciousness; the bursting forward from within, after all the moisture in the log has completely dried and the temperature reaches a critical level, is the higher consciousness coming forward. Inside, we already are spiritual and the external personality has to align with the internal- then there is personal enlightenment. Which according to tradition is not a static condition; higher knowledge comes and goes, depending upon the requirements of the situation.*

*Within each spiritual framework there are exercises, prayers, and books to read; these form the external activity, or heat of the fire that the traveler adds to their day and life. The inner or spiritual effects of this activity, gradually builds upon the soul, such as the opening of specific spiritual centers or chakras, and comes forward naturally. Through the twin action of this activity, one day, suddenly the log bursts open, aflame, both from inner and external heat.*

*Now, in order to help travelers further understand how to add spirituality into their daily routine, turning life into a prayer; which is the goal of Sufi spiritual development, let's talk about everyday spirituality and some practical ways to add this dimension.*

Sure, why not?

*Our culture is participating in an explosion of new age teaching, interest in eastern religion, and a general curiosity about the usefulness of everyday spiritual practice. When you turn on the television, it seems just about every talk show host is discussing how to maximize human potential and help viewers become a more advanced version of self.*

*In our effort to reach higher, spirituality is a major interest in the books we read, the classes we take, and inner peace we all want to find. Accordingly, there is growing dialogue concerning differences between traditional religious teaching and a form of spiritual practice termed: everyday spirituality or spirituality of the market place. Interestingly enough, the usefulness of spiritual practice in everyday life is an ancient teaching, and lies at the heart of human development systems like Sufism; where travelers are taught, through ordinary daily activity, to align with the higher and make life a prayer.*

> Religion may be compared
> To a great river that feeds the land.
> The River winds its way as a mighty force
> And smaller tributaries are formed
> To serve the distant regions.
> Some are satisfied
> To drink of the small stream
> And forget they must travel
> The river to its Source.
>
> Beyond the river's gate
> The Ocean is waiting.

S.B.

*For spiritual travelers, at some point, it becomes clear that new age and eastern systems offer techniques that speak to the basic difference between religious form and personal spiritual experience. While all traditional religious systems are based upon spiritual teachings, inner personal experience is not always emphasized and many travelers leave the religion of their birth with a deep, inner hunger that religious form did not completely fill.*

Like in my case...

*Exactly. In the beginning stages of any learning, adherence to form is essential; and as the traveler matures in their traditional religious training, a deeper more personal experience may be available. However, many travelers leave for a variety of reasons and get 'turned-off' long before this happens.*

*In viewing traditional religious teaching and spiritual experience, it is important to discuss the difference between internal and external reality. Most of us are familiar with the external form of religious teaching; usually this was the presentation offered during our early childhood and emphasized standard prayers, teachings and social prescription which was directed at a large segment of humanity.*

*Over the centuries, this is the part that looks different, because it is different and it changes; external form varies depending upon culture, geography, historical context, and the changing needs of the receiving community. Because this part is not the same, and is tied to time and place, it confuses people; this is the part that travelers argue and fight about. Yet, internally all forms at their highest level are one, united in spirit.*

*The internal or spiritual essence, which gives life to the external religious form, is a living, vibrant element. This part, termed the Light in our presentation, is the inner core or life current to the eternal form. This is the part that fuels the updating of the teaching into a newer presentation, and the grace that enables the living teacher or exemplar to function. This is the spiritual essence the new age traveler seeks to embrace, and become one with.*

Religion is like a beautiful maiden, who to fit the changing weather, wears an assortment of clothing. Some days, because the weather is cold or sunny, her outer garments are different. If you were to describe her on these days, one day she would be the maiden in the tall woolen hat, scarf across her face and long coat, and on another day, the women in the light, bright, yellow cotton dress. On the first day, not seeing her covered face, some observers might be fooled and argue or disagree about the women's identity or description on the second day; not realizing underneath the various clothing, it is the same young women wearing the light cotton dress.

S.B.

*For the most part, everyday activity, work, and worry block the inner awareness from coming forward. When focusing on daily life, the 'noise' or vibration of this activity prevents the inner awareness from being accessed and perceived. As we've touched on before, with training, travelers can be taught to operate both streams of consciousness simultaneously. However, this is not a static condition; the capacity to tune in and use the higher consciousness, comes and goes, depending upon the traveler's capacity and higher needs of the situation.*

*The goal of spiritual paths is to add a measure of conscious, spiritual awareness to the traveler's individual life; this awareness serves as an enriching, enabling element so the traveler can complete daily and higher functions. Each traveler is unique, and as such has an individual life plan, which ultimately leads them to join in as co-creator, helping to influence their own and the higher destiny of others. Traditionally, in this earth realm, the completed person is God's deputy or vicegerent.*

*Next, why don't you give another, practical example on how to turn daily worry and fear into a spiritual exercise?*

I thought you would never stop talking! Thanks for finally letting me get a word in!

*Touchy. Touchy.*

Anyway. Here are 2 teaching encounters with Sam on how to turn negative self-talk, worry, and selfish preoccupation into something higher. Often, when consumed with personal worry and fear; thoughts become tiresome, time consuming, and run through a repetitive, sometimes depressing, pattern. As indicated earlier, a positive way to break this cycle is to get-up and do something for someone else.

### Action Teaching

Upon entering Sam's Office, it was his custom to offer guests coffee or tea. On this particular day, after Zach, Eddy and I sat down, Sam looked directly at Eddy and ordered: "Make me a cup of coffee. I want the perfect cup of coffee." Sam rarely spoke in this manner, and hardly ever ordered students to do anything. Nervously Eddy got up and made his way to the table, wondering, what was a perfect cup of coffee? While pouring, Eddy inquired as to how Sam liked his coffee. Then Eddy prepared the cup and offered it to Sam. After sipping, Sam said, it needed more milk and sugar. So, Eddy went back and nervously added additional milk and sugar. This time, when Sam sipped the drink, he said, "Aah a perfect cup of coffee."

During the time Eddy was preparing the coffee, we could see that he was anxious and relieved when Sam finally accepted the 'perfect cup.'

This event was not followed by any explanation. After we left the office, we all were excited about what it meant. We couldn't figure it out and it is only time which has given me some indication of the multi-level meaning.

Another incident which helps illustrate one point that Sam was trying to make, occurred another day when Steve was visiting. Steve was complaining how badly life was treating him (this was something we all did from time to time), and Sam told Steve to make breakfast for his family on weekends. Sam instructed to get up bright and early and make the foods everyone in his family liked.

On the surface, how does this exchange add up? Here we have someone who is complaining about their life and the prescription is to do something for someone else. Sam believed the body thrived on activity and needed to be used in a constructive manner for physical and mental health. This was Steve's prescription: stop worrying so much about self and contribute to the greater good, i.e., make breakfast.

Both Steve's and Eddy's story are related in that an action was prescribed for a psychological condition. For the spiritual traveler, psychological states must be stabilized before work can begin on spiritual ones. In both situations, Sam felt that the student was spending too much time thinking about self. So, the prescription was to do something for someone else. Also, while doing something for someone else, feelings of mastery occur and physical activity is a healthy antidote to milder forms of depression. Sam used to say: 'the mind is so constructed that it can only keep one thing in it at a time.'

So, if you're busy making the perfect cup of coffee, you can't be worrying about yourself; and in the alchemy of the situation every one benefits. Try it for yourself and see if it can really be that simple.

## Sam Saying

Why are you unhappy? You are always in the Presence of God.

\*     \*

# — 14 —

# Our Conversation Draws to a Close – Parting Words for the Road

The breath that does not repeat the name of God is a wasted breath.

Kabir

How about we continue by offering a set of beliefs, or creed of sorts that the spiritual traveler can follow daily?

*Sure. What a great idea! Why don't you continue; we can take turns. After you finish the first part, I'll jump in, as we alternate. Also, before starting I think we need to point out that some of the guideline material is repetitive however we feel it is important enough to require restating.*

Now, may I begin?

*Not another word until it's my turn...*

According to tradition, humanity originated 'far beyond the stars' and is on a journey back to its Source. While in the earth phase, there are numerous opportunities to embrace 'our real' or 'lasting nature,' and begin the spiritual journey home. In this physical world, because we are in a sense estranged from our real or lasting spiritual nature, there is an unease and inner hunger that pushes us forward to search and make the inner connection.

While in this world, many become distracted and attempt to fill the inner emptiness with all manner of things and experiences; this further compounds the problem of remembering who we are.

Just like ET in the movie, we need to contact home, through our inner spiritual awareness, so the energies might align and we can start the return journey.

Now, while in the earth phase, because of its endless diversity, beauty and splendor, each traveler has the opportunity to create and freely join with the Creator. Daily, we create our own multiple level realities and we create multiple opportunities to express who we are. Inside each of us is a spark or piece of the Life Force; that is our guiding element and leads us through the many worlds, back to the Creator.

*O spiritual traveler, rise up and know who you really are; temporarily shed the identity that has been placed upon you by others and this wondrous physical body we have created. On some levels, this multi-level form is an illusion, a contrast and story, created to help, hurt, contain and even set us free. Although many were well intentioned, they were fooled by this riddle of physicality and spirituality; ultimately, this contrast and duality exists to help, so we may learn, experience and enjoy the wonders. Yes, we may create and experience it all, as long as we remember; go deep within and experience who we really are- a child of Light.*

*The present life and experience is all about you, and what you individually wish to create. That is the wonder and challenge; we were given free will so that we might freely choose to remember and join in the creative process: alternating between our will and the will of the One.*

*Perhaps this is confusing? O spiritual traveler; set yourself free and stop thinking about it all. Go deeper than the intellect will allow and learn to experience and perceive your true lasting nature; you and the Light are one. This oneness will set you free so you may create that which you came here to create. Enough of riddles and words that make little sense and cannot be thought out. Arise and embrace your lasting self; then the foolishness of words will no longer be necessary.*

Beyond religion, beyond individual creed and spiritual form, there is a knowing that arises from the heart. The heart is our spiritual center, and is connected to the Light or life force; the Light is most like the creator and, while in the physical body, is the conduit through which we travel home. Make your life a song, a celebration through which you reach higher and embrace your spiritual heritage.

Come, join me as a spiritual traveler; a traveler who seeks the inner, spiritual core of religious experience and follows the Light through the many worlds. This way has always existed...It is the religion before there was religion. It is the first commandment: *Love God (or the Light) with all your heart and soul.* Yes, it is as easy as that...

And because we are in the world of forms, we need a structure or framework from which to begin; here for the spiritual traveler, is a set of guidelines that have served me well. These guidelines are not of my creation, but part of the wondrous path that has always existed; like a scribe I write them down so you might learn, experience and benefit.

And if you think I am a madman, and have lost my way, leave this writing and find your own experience and way to embrace your true lasting self. One way is not better than others. Each is a child of the universe; and each must ultimately find their own way, that is both unique and the same. For we all are travelers. May your journey be glorious and your effort rewarded.

- *Love God.* This is the first commandment and basically summarizes the entire journey-, which is to *Love God (or the Light) with all your heart and soul.* Some need no other instruction; traditionally, these travelers have been called the lovers. The lovers seek to make their lives an extension of the divine and do everything for their beloved.

- *Citizen of the Universe.* Learn to share this planet and the universe with all the many life forms; we are all expressions of the one. To hurt another is to hurt self; we all are connected in spirit. We share the same life force. When we turn toward the Light, the Light will guide and protect.

- *Align With the Highest.* In each action and thought, seek to take the high road and make every moment an expression of the divine. Listen to your heart and make your decisions based upon that which will serve your higher nature and the emerging higher destiny of the universe.

- *Love Another.* The nature of God or the Light is pure love; when we love another and seek to help and share with that person; we are fulfilling our higher destiny. Many of the ills of the world come about because travelers are fearful and seek to fulfill their own need at the expense of others. Mature travelers know the difference between helping and hurting; their hearts will not let them intentionally cause harm.

- *Live Fully.* Each traveler is a multi-level being with an assortment of feelings, thoughts, desires, and dreams. Live fully and embrace the many parts of self. Also, do not forget to go deeper and thank the One who gave these things to you.

- *Seek Excellence.* In every action and thought seek to do your best. Each traveler has the potential to reach toward excellence; each has a unique skill set and must learn to maximize their potential by expressing individual talents and ability. A complete life merges individual and higher need.

- *Be Yourself.* In knowing who you are, you will know the many parts of self and merge with the higher. Do not let others keep you from finding out and expressing who you are; that is your gift to yourself and the universe.

- *Help Others.* In helping others, we serve the highest. Though we may sometimes forget, we are all one, and have a social duty to help others of our human family. No one is suggesting that we are not to care for self or protect self, however, everyone is connected and on the higher, spiritual level, when my neighbor is hungry or sick, I am experiencing this as well.

- *Do Good Deeds.* Inwardly, the healthy person knows what's right; we are born with this inner awareness. It is only our fear that blocks us from doing the right thing in any given situation; learn to go beyond fear and listen to your heart. Then the promise of a better world will be achieved one person at a time.

- *Gratitude.* Thank the universe, thank yourself, and thank the creator for all you have been given. This activity will make you joyous, and its energy will fill you with good health.

- *Pray.* Each morning and evening, and throughout the day: communicate and speak with God. Have an ongoing conversation with your higher self and the one who provided you with all the opportunities of this lifetime. One of my teachers used to say, 'if you're going to be angry or sad, be angry or sad with God. Similarly, if you're going to be happy, be happy with God. When we are most distant from God that is when we need God the most."

- *Travel Beyond Teachings.* All we know about any great servant and their specific teachings is what others have recorded, wanting us to know about these teachings. This is both good and bad. That is why each traveler is urged to have their own experience and travel beyond teachings. Knowledge is different than teachings.

*

Pray for the things you want
but work for the things you need.

Modern Traditional

*

Love is bestowed, not earned.

Al-Hujwiri

\* \*

*Well, we're just about at the end of our conversation. Have you enjoyed our journey together? In this discussion, we have expressed ourselves and these shifting patterns are offered as a potential framework to help you travel within and solve the maze of your own consciousness.*

Finally, some advice for travelers who are searching for a teacher: if there is a path or teacher that interests you, first, familiar yourself with that path or teacher's work. Usually, for further study, advance or preparatory materials have been offered to help get you ready. Then, contact that teacher or path's representative and request instruction.

Looking back, we have tried to accomplish the following:

- Offer an insider's view of what takes place in two modern spiritual or mystical schools. While this might not be your experience or experience reported by others, it serves as "food for thought," hopefully, that will inspire, teach and lead you forward.

- Some attempt has been made to show how spiritual learning can be integrated into daily life. For that is the point of spiritual learning; being useful in ordinary life.

- Finally, we live in an age where it is apparent that humanity now has the means to destroy itself; hopefully, this will not occur, and one of the deterrents to this happening is to create better people who use all of their talents to make the world better. To help in solving the world's problems, our perspective is: the missing ingredient is spiritual capacity; used along

138

side all other capacities, in a holistic, integrated manner. At this point in history, our world requires a spirituality that transcends individual creed and religion and calls to our common bond. We are all children of the Light, and reach our full potential when we seek the highest in each moment, treating our neighbor as ourselves.

Traditionally, when the traveler departs, as a form of hospitality, a gift or supplies are provided for the next part of the journey. Now, let me leave you with a fable; it is about a magical child who touches the lives of many with a simple lesson.

May this story be an additional blessing to you, and help you reach higher. Until we meet again.

\*       \*

## — 15 —

# Story: The Star Child

## Day - I

The people suffered. Long had it been a time of fear and darkness. All of the old ways had been tested and each failed. Greed consumed the lawmakers and Masters of Business. Their decisions turned against them and the once great structures of finance and service lay in the ashes of burnt dreams.

After the collapse of government and halls of finance, the Generals took control and worked toward order. Gradually, goods and services were restored. However, this system too was filled with graft and long delays. Even under the Generals, the rich got richer and the people worked long hours to feed their family.

After the graft, little was left for the people. Their hearts cried out for deliverance and freedom from the struggle of their daily lives and empty promises. Over time, the Masters of Religion had taken to hiding in the shadows, fearful the people would turn against them, blaming them for the chaos and destruction. Had not the old prophecy come to pass? Was not the world in disarray and darkness? All could see greed and fear consumed the land. People from one sector turned against the people of another. Nightly, mothers cried as their children lay in their beds with swollen, empty bellies.

Lost in despair, most had forgotten the second part of the prophecy. From the ashes, The Deliverer would appear. On an inner level, the people's hearts called out for justice and redemption.

Where was the One who would lead them from the darkness into the Light?

From the people's heart, the Deliverer was reborn. The people's suffering called forth her arrival. This was the time. This was the place.

*        *        *        *        *

As the moonlight glistened across the sand and the stars lit the night, the Star Child walked toward the town square. Each evening, the young people gathered to talk, play and socialize. Here the young ones had a few minutes of enjoyment away from the drudgery of their lives and the world their parents created. Dreams for tomorrow could be shared between friends and enthusiasm met with the thrill of expectation. In the hearts of the young, lay the foundation for the New World. Instinctively, the young knew there was both a collective and individual destiny. Greed made people forget we were our brother's keeper and filled each with fear about their personal tomorrow.

Slowly, the Star Child inhaled the cool evening air and listened to the crickets singing to the evening. It had been a long time since she walked on this planet. There were many worlds and much work to be done. Here, The Great Cycle was completing and the Star Child was the final spoke in the wheel. Hope was to replace despair and renewal to replace decay. This was the beginning. This was the rebirth.

*        *        *        *        *

Before entering the town square, the Star Child paused and gazed upward at the evening sky. As she said a silent prayer, she smiled at the thousands of shining stars decorating the ebony ceiling. These points of light called to the light within. Darkness and Light were brothers; part of the greater whole of the universe. Each person was part of this. Each particle within was part of the fabric of Darkness and Light. Each was comprised of the very substance of the stars and once this was perceived, the corrective was added. In time, this corrective led to right action.

141

During the course of each life, there were opportunities to re-member and reach higher, joining the stars as a brother. Each per-son was part of this universal fabric and yearned to travel upward to fulfill their destiny.

In this world, the pull was in two directions: one toward the earth and one toward the heavens. When the balance was destroyed and earthly concerns blocked spiritual ones, the Star Child was sent. The people's pain and suffering called her forth. She was the uni-versal bringer of Light. She was the beacon for the stormy night and came to restore balance.

\*      \*      \*      \*      \*

As the young talked and laughed, deep inside many understood much was missing. Yes, it was fun to be with friends. Laughter and song were necessary, but how was their inner emptiness and pain to be eased? Something told these young, life was more than working, playing and struggling for food. Instinctively, many felt that to join the takers and give in to the world of greed was no solution to the alternative of not having enough. Were these the only choices?

And the inner voice continued to whisper: "What of the heart and the longing of the soul to reach higher?"

Because this was a Dark Age, some young had taken to strik-ing out against authority and those who disagreed with them. In their view, pain begot pain. For them, the solution resided in be-ing strong and beating the takers at their game. These young roved in packs, using violence as a way to fill their lives. Covering their pain with anger and destruction, they took what they wanted and contributed to the darkness of the times.

\*      \*      \*      \*      \*

Born of the people's need, the Star Child appeared as one of them. Coming to heal the pain of those most injured, she walked as a young teenage girl. With silver blond hair, skin of light olive, eyes of ocean blue, just under five feet of height, she walked effortlessly across the sand, emanating peace and stillness. Calling first to the young, gradually, her message would reach out to everyone. All were in need of healing, but none more than these. Their futures were consumed by the sickness of greed and fear that filled the land.

And when she walked into that gathering of young people and took her place among them, at first, none recognized who she was. Gradually, as the Light danced about her and reached out into the darkness, touching the hearts of those gathered, they began to realize she was the answer to their hopes. Here, was the beacon for the dark night and the exemplar to follow.

Even in this day, the Star Child's words from that gathering call to the child who is free and loving in us. Rise up as an aware soul. Make your place in the evening sky and embrace the opportunity to join the stars as kin.

*      *      *      *      *

"O children of the darkness, I have come to lead you home. I am the fruit of your suffering and the ointment for your tired soul."

"Long have you cried and long have you searched. Yet, the solution to your problem is inside of you. I have come to display it to you and help you embrace your own higher destiny."

"In many ways, with your thoughts you create your own world and have been taught to think and act only in certain ways. Daily, these ways must be pushed aside for a time and you must learn again to perceive your own Inner Light and stillness. For this light is the light of the heavens and connects you to all things. You have forgotten, you are a star, which began in a distant galaxy and one day must return home. While in this world, you must put time aside to remember and honor your spiritual heritage. This remembrance is the balancing factor and, in this age, has been lost and forgotten."

"Because of the pull toward the earth and the need for material expression, it is natural to be tied to the world. Yet, you are also a child of the heavens and must learn to awaken and use your spiritual capacity. Then the balance between the earth and stars will be restored."

*      *      *      *      *

The youngest of those gathered began to speak. "Who are you? Why do you speak to us in this way? Why should we believe anything you say? You are just a child like us."

The Star Child smiled, slowly looked at all who were gathered and replied.

"Can't you feel it? It is the pull of the stars...My words travel on the energy of the universe and while words are necessary to convince you intellectually, you can also feel the energy within the words. Embrace this energy. It is your home and is the Source who sent me here."

"I am the child of your longing. On a cold night, I am the brother to keep you warm and the sister with whom to whisper your secrets. In each, there is emptiness, a hunger that waits to be filled by the Light of Eternity. In this age, many have sought to fill this hunger with all kinds of material things. They have sought the things of the earth to quiet the universal desire for things of the spirit. Greed has blinded them to their own higher nature and they fumble around in the dark like a blindfolded fool."

"Listen to my words and think about them. Perceive the energy and love that support the words. Question what I say. Deep inside, you will recognize the call of Truth. This call reaches out and heals the emptiness and loneliness inside you. It embraces the part that wants to make sense out of the pain and suffering in the world. To know and to believe that there is a higher purpose. This is something you must decide for yourself. I have come to present this opportunity and offer a solution. Only you can decide to accept or reject it."

Then another questioned, "Where did you come from? You call yourself the child of our longing. What exactly does that mean? What you say is in the form of riddles. The words sound grand but their meaning is vague."

"I have come from a place far away. So far away that it may be said, it is beyond the stars. I am a traveler who has been sent here to bring the corrective. The balance has been disturbed and I have come to restore that which has been lost. In this age, people have forgotten they are both children of the earth and children of the stars. Both parts of their nature must be honored and developed. The pain and suffering of this time has called me forth. Like a magnet, I have been pulled into this realm to offer hope and a way to restore the balance."

"You too are children of spirit and must learn to soar upward claiming your place in the evening sky. Tell your friends I have come. Invite them here to question and listen. Each evening I will be here so all of you will learn anew to perceive your higher nature. Listen to my words, evaluate them, travel on their energy and go deep within. This energy calls to the part of you that is a star child and will live on forever. Until this energy is awakened in each of you this world will be a dark place, filled with fear and greed."

"The corrective for the dark night is Light. I am the bringer of this Light and serve another who is its Origin. Tell your friends, hope has been awakened and has come to balance the darkness of the long night."

*     *     *     *     *

Again the youngest questioned, "Who are you? I still don't understand who you are." And with a smile on her face, the Star Child said, "Look into my eyes. I will show you who I am."

Slowly, as the crowd looked into the Star Child's eyes, her eyes began to sparkle and grow brighter. And as the young ones gazed deeper, the two orbs of brilliance began to expand becoming two blue, green oceans that were ablaze with a brilliant sunrise. And as this energy, emanating from her eyes grew stronger gradually all they could see was brilliance and light. Then the darkness of the evening sky was consumed by light. Many had to shield their eyes and turn away.

Suddenly, the light disappeared and the Star Child was gone.

At first blinded by the brilliance, the young ones fumbled about unable to see. Then as their sight returned, each silently walked home, and their hearts were filled with joy and hope.

*       *       *       *       *

## Day - II

It was the second night and more young people had come to question and learn from the Star Child. Among the young, word quickly spread of the messenger of Light and the town square was filled. Many had come hoping to be part of something greater than themselves. Others came to learn, and others came because they had nothing else to do.

As the anticipation and excitement grew, some of those gathered began to wonder if the Star Child would keep her word and appear a second time. The appointed hour was growing near and there was no sign of her walking across the sands. On the previous evening, this was the direction of her approach and expectantly eyes focused toward the western sands.

As the clock in the town square struck 7 pm, the Star Child appeared. Miraculously, she materialized from amongst the crowd. One moment there were groups of young people softly talking to each other, then a flash of light, which startled everyone and gradually she took form seemingly from the very air itself. Tiny particles of glimmering light rushed together and, in a moment, she was reborn.

Startled, the crowd was quiet and fixed their eyes upon her, wondering what next might happen. Amidst the wonder of this moment, some of the younger children began to grow nervous; sensing the fear, the Star Child addressed the crowd.

"O children of the dark night do not be fearful. I am one of you and have come to restore hope. I have been sent by One who loves you more than you can ever know. This is the hour when all your questions will have answers and all your fears will be replaced by love. Let the questioning begin."

Then a young girl, no more than four years old, who was standing next to where the Star Child appeared, called out, "I am frightened. The people in our village do not travel about as you. My brother and his friends say you are a witch or a magician. I am frightened. Please do not hurt me."

146

Gently, the Star Child gazed at the young one, smiled and whispered, "I would not hurt you, you are my sister and the reason that I have come." Taking in this reply, tentatively, the young girl put aside her fear and returned the smile.

Looking up and turning toward the larger crowd, the Star Child commanded, "Now, bring to me your questions."

With a challenge in his voice, a tall teenager shouted from the middle of the crowd. "You say that you are one of us. Yet, how can that be? None of us travel about like you or have the powers that you appear to have. Why should we trust you?"

With a smile on her face, the Star Child replied, "Sometimes, you have to trust your heart. You must listen to your heart's whisper and believe that events will turn out for the best. It is good that you question. Your mind wonders, how can this girl, if she is indeed a girl, be like one of us? She looks like us, but she is clearly different with a strength and awareness that we do not have."

"Know that we are the same. We have the same Source. The One who Created this world and universe. Our Source has sent me here to help. Also, I am what you will become. I am that spark which is deep inside you and lives on; taking you through the many worlds. I am the accumulated energy of many hearts burning for freedom."

Again, the same teenage boy called, "Even if we were to accept what you say, why have you come to us? In this world of takers, we are nothing."

"Because the Source has a message for you. The Source says, "This world is more than it appears. Remember, the race does not always go to the strongest or bravest. Sometimes, it goes to the one who hears the higher call and cannot be shaken." The Source says, "If you will take one step toward me, I will take ten toward you. This is the hour of change, but before the change can be enacted, you must be prepared."

Then, the young girl called out, "Please, tell us more about the One who sent you, and if love be his way, why has our world fallen into darkness?"

"Because in order for there to be light; there must be darkness. What good is the sunrise without the ebony covering of the night sky? Both these opposites exist so you may travel beyond them. I am here to show you what supports this world of forms. By connecting with this underlying reality, each of you will reach higher, remember and take the next step in your personal evolution."

Another youth, who was quickly reaching manhood, called out, "Enough with words. All of the adults in our world use words to make promises that have become empty. We need something more than words and promises. What do you have to say to that?"

"Tonight I will give you experience and show you what you each will become. By focusing inward, I will display to you, your own inner potential and you will consciously connect with the creative energy that is your Origin. But first, each of you must promise something. Will you promise me?"

"And what might that be?" shouted back voices from the crowd.

"That you must talk about this and share this experience with everyone you know. Each of you must tell your parents, friends, and classmates. Tonight when you go back to your homes, you must use your computers and telephones and ask these people to speak with everyone they know about it. Can you do this?"

Growing excited, the crowd of young people called back, "Yes."

"Good," called the Star Child. "Now, I want you all to sit down; if you are already seated, then stay where you are." Slowly, as the great crowd found a place to sit, the Star Child waited.

"Next, I want you all to take a deep breath and hold onto the air with your lungs; breathe in through your nose and embrace the evening air. Feel its coolness and smell its sweetness. You are part of this wondrous beauty. Now, hold your breath and exhale very slowly through your mouth. Feel the air as it leaves your lungs returning to the greater world. Now, let us repeat this breathing exercise."

Together, the great crowd repeated the timeless motion of going out and returning. In this way, gradually, they grew calmer and more familiar with following the Star Child's soothing voice. As she spoke, her voice was a gentle whisper that even the most distant participant could hear; a soft melody, like peaceful water caressing the children, running across the night air.

"Next, I want you to close your eyes and focus inward. Do not be afraid. While I am here no one can harm you. Trust me. Close your eyes. Focus inward and picture a ball of white light. See this orb, in your mind's eye, pulsating with clear, white, peaceful energy. This light calls to you and is part of you."

"If your mind strays, and another thought enters, do not fight it; simply return to your ball of white light. This is a thought form you are creating in your mind's eye; it is yours and is part of you. Now, as the light pulsates with its peaceful energy pattern, feel this energy as it flows through your body and awareness. Slowly, you and this light must join and become one..."

And as the Star Child's voice led the children along the ancient and universal path of spiritual awakening, she took the Light from the ether and focused it upon all the individual orbs that were aglow in each child's heart. Then, because of the Star Child's intervention, as each individual light grew brighter and stronger, it split apart. One portion stayed within the child, as each child remained seated in the town square, and another portion journeyed upward into the night's sky. Finding its own place in the heavens, each child was now a star to illume the darkness and shared its light across the heavens.

In that timeless moment that part of each child seated below offered up its innermost hope in the form of a prayer. Miraculously, each prayer was answered, in the form of a personal dream, showing the children what still was possible with their lives.

Later, as the crowd broke up and dispersed, each child was aglow with the hope of a brighter tomorrow. As they walked toward their homes, filled with renewed energy, children spoke to each other about what they experienced. Fantastically, while each had the same experience of being a star in the evening sky; no two shared the same dream, or personal wish for the future. Each life varied, full of possibilities and opportunities to create something more.

\*       \*       \*       \*       \*

As the children promised, that evening, when they got home they shared their experiences with everyone who would listen. Phone calls, text messages and e-mails were sent out all across the world. Such was the thrill and the excitement of that hour. In a hundred homes, incredulously, parents listened to little ones relating stories about becoming a shining star and describing in detail their personal, bright future that lay ahead. It had been years since so much hope had entered so many places at once.

\*     \*     \*     \*     \*

## Day - III

And the next day, when the children went to school, all were abuzz about the night before and what the Star Child said and did. Quickly, the local news picked up on this story and features were being aired on television and radio stations. Also, scores of meetings were held in halls of government, among the Generals and Masters of Religion. Debates raged how these events might alter their control of the people, and they began to strategize so this would not happen.

\*     \*     \*     \*     \*

It was time. Again, the Star Child materialized on the sands that bordered the town and felt their coolness underfoot as she walked effortlessly toward the square. Even at this distance, she could hear the noise and felt the many people, adults and children, who were waiting. Their combined energy was stronger that the previous evenings, with greater variability and shades of darkness. This was all part of the Plan and the inevitable outcome so that the Teaching might again manifest. She was but a vehicle and joyfully embraced her role.

Understanding there were too many people to pass through to reach the center of the square, she willed herself there. In an instant, she was standing beside the fountain, enjoying the cool spray of the water upon her skin and dress. Night had come to the surrounding countryside, but here in the middle of this great crowd of people, the lights from the TV cameras and their large companion spotlights made it seem like day. Much like an actress who enters upon a stage, she waited for the crowd to acknowledge her presence. Then, a young a boy called, "Look. She has come. We told you, she was real."

In an instant, the cameras and their lights turned and further illuminated where she stood. Then, a young female reporter quickly moved forward and offered a microphone into which the Star Child could speak. The Star Child looked at the reporter and shook her head, indicating that this would not be necessary. With anticipation, every head turned and waited. On this night, they wondered, what would be revealed?

*      *      *      *      *

On the roof of the tallest building that bordered the town square, General Gates gave his crack sniper team final instructions. These two marksmen were the very best and had never failed in each of their many missions. This night, they were teamed together so there would be no doubt as to outcome. Earlier in the day, it was decided unanimously in a joint meeting between the Generals and the Masters of Religion, there would be no more gatherings and fantastic stories to ignite and impassion the young. Hope and optimism were to be replaced with order and control; several well-placed bullets to the head would ensure this.

*      *      *      *      *

"In my journey to this world, this time, I brought my message to the young children. It is they who are the hope for the future and most receptive to this teaching's form. This time, I showed you the Source. This creative, life giving energy of which you all have a piece in your heart will help lead you back home..."

Suddenly, there was a twin explosion. "Crack! Crack!" Simultaneously, the snipers had released their bullets and before anyone could turn in the direction of the terrible sound, the Star Child disappeared. As the bullets raced to where she was standing, the Star

Child was gone. In her place was a great balled figure of pulsating Light. The luminescence of this great 10-foot high ball of Blue White Light dwarfed the brightness output of the many TV Cameras and spotlights. Somehow, as the bullets passed into this lighted orb, they were absorbed and the ball grew even stronger.

Then, as the crowd realized someone had just tried to shoot and kill the Star Child, the great ball of Light began to ascend from the ground and slowly rise into the night sky. And as this Light grew brighter, it rested and hovered just above the town square. As a final message, these were the words spoken, in her kind, gentle voice:

*"On the night when you are low and filled with despair, look to the evening sky for I will be the brightest star there."*

And as many tears began to fall, like a racing comet, the Star Child rose and filled the night sky with a long trail of Light, returning to her place, as the brightest star amidst the milky-way galaxy.

\*　　\*　　\*　　\*　　\*

In the years that followed, the hundreds of children that personally experienced the Star Child's message grew into adulthood and gradually took their rightful place as leaders in the larger world about them. And as the older generation passed away, these children of hope and change sang the praises of the Star Child by making their world a brighter place.

And in this land, it has remained a custom, that upon seeing the first star of the evening, each child sings the traditional song and makes a wish for their future.

\*

Be the change you wish
To see in the world.

Gandhi

— A —

# Article: The Mystical School

## By Dr. Stewart Bitkoff

### Introduction

In today's spiritual market place there are many options. The student wishing to complete their spiritual journey is faced with different choices; often selecting learning experience which appeals to them, thereby missing other essential elements and failing to benefit from a complete system. Because the student thinks he/she can direct their own study or make a choice about which path to follow, the journey is often flawed from the start. While spiritual schools are similar to other forms of learning and past traditional learning experience is helpful, there are different or spiritual parameters which effect outcome. Most often the potential student is unaware of these and simply feels about in the dark.

The purpose of this discussion is to help the student understand some of the factors involved in the operation and selection process of a mystical school.

### Selectivity

Before beginning, first the student must accept a humbling fact. In this area of inquiry, most ordinary rules do not apply and generally students have a limited understanding of how mystical schools operate. These schools are unlike other classroom situations or seminars that one takes. In these, if we are interested in the course of study, we apply to be accepted and meeting entry requirements, we pay our fees and begin. In some ways, these learning experiences are set-up like a business. The more students, the most gain for everyone. The assumption being, with correct preparation and desire, most students can benefit from what is being taught.

Yet, mystical schools are not set up this way. They are very selective. You cannot gain entrance by applying for admission because you are interested. There must be an inner call which the Teacher or Master perceives in the student. This the Master does through inner spiritual cognition. This call, or higher impulse operating in the student, is the basic element that gives the school life and vibrancy; also, it is this elemental energy that the Master connects with to perceive, teach and function. In fact, the goal of the mystical process and the work of the entire school are the refinement and use of this elemental spiritual energy. The student meets the entrance requirement if this capacity is already at a sufficient level where it can be called forth and further developed. Additionally, the student must be leading a balanced life, free of limiting emotional disorder and part of the society in which they live. While spiritual capacity is in everyone, often, it is not ready to be worked on in a beneficial way. In most, this capacity is covered over by 'the dust of selfish living' and the student has work to do before this element can be refined by the school. To begin prematurely can harm the student and create imbalance.

Second, most mystical schools which specialize in the refinement of this higher impulse/energy are hidden. Generally, they do not take out advertisements in the local newspaper inviting applicants. Often, they do not look like schools with classrooms and buildings set aside for learning. They might take the form of a business, a professional society, be in a hospital, or a local highway department. The meetings might be held in someone's home after work or in their office during lunch. Learning might be transmitted spiritually while the student is sleeping or while they are working. The student might be told to continue their normal routine of work and play and read a series of books. They might be directed to enroll in a correspondence course and given selected pieces to read and comment upon.

In this model, ordinary life is the classroom, the course of study is specific to the student and study is directed by a Master. Here there is a minimum of time away from others. The end product being a completed person; one who has added refined spiritual capacity and is better able to serve in their community. Students are taught to participate in the world and help make it a better place.

## The Master Knows

The completed person, who is Master or Guide, is able to show the way to potential students, because they have traveled the path themselves. The Master has completed the journey, that is, reached a high degree of spiritual development and has been given permission to teach and guide others. Not everyone is needed to do this. In the spiritual hierarchy, there are many functions and duties. Teacher-ship is one function and set of responsibilities.

Most students feel they can determine a Master by the way he/she speaks, makes them feel or by the powers displayed. Yet, it is the spirit as liberated that knows the true Master. Like calls to like and the Master embraces the student's heart, located in the Spirit- setting it free. The Grace of the Path is the enabling energy factor; acting as a nutrient to release the student's inner spiritual capacity. Other characteristics of the Master include: an overriding concern for the student's well being; provision of an individual course of study specific to the student which is varied with general practices for everyone; and the capacity to provide everything the student needs to reach spiritual completion.

The Master exists because of the student's need. Both benefit from this interaction and form a strong bond. This is a spiritual bond and the Master's primary responsibility is to show the student their own latent inner capacity and how to refine it. Without a Master few would reach higher; getting lost in the mire of self-deception, struggle for spiritual powers, and false teachings.

The Master can teach in any format. All things have an aspect of the Divine and the Master is able to show this to the student. Depending upon the culture and the needs of the people, the format will vary. In our culture, psychological, self-help, improved health and scientific vehicles are currently being employed.

## Filling the Emptiness

Deep within, the student has a hunger, an emptiness, which can only be filled by the Light of Eternity. This 'great hunger' leads people in all kinds of directions and has been described as a burning desire, restlessness or unease. It is an inborn spiritual need and most people try to fill this primal hunger with secondary phenomena. Because of this action, they are never truly satisfied and rarely accept the primal emptiness for what it is. Sadly, many spend much of their lives never satisfied, seeking a variety of secondary phenomena, always looking in the wrong direction.

The Master calls to those students who are able to perceive this unease as a spiritual need. These students, because of an inner sincerity, or latent degree of spiritual capacity, quickly connect with the Master's call, thereby defining the inner hunger. This initial caress, felt in the heart, is an initiation by the Master into the mystical school. Spiritually, the Master caresses the student with the Light of Eternity and the student is accepted. This is an inner knowing which both the student and Master share; it is life changing and becomes the yardstick for future experience. The essence of the school and its course work is to refine the capacity to perceive this spiritual energy. The student is taught this through the initial spiritual caress.

In the journey to spiritual completion, the learning is without end. Many are the spiritual experiences and lessons. Quickly, the student learns these experiences and higher capacities are provided to make the student a better person who is more fully equipped to serve their community. This is a natural, gradual process of learning and the student is expected to maintain all areas of daily life becoming more responsible. Spiritual responsibilities are in addition to other duties.

Rarely, in this school, is a student asked to live apart from others and or not participate in the affairs of the world. If this occurs, it is for a short period and to teach something specific. All human capacities, skills, and abilities are needed to make the world better. Spiritual capacity is one aspect of a healthy, more complete life; serving as center from which other capacities emanate.

### Spiritual Hierarchy

The Path consists of the Master, students, Spiritual Hierarchy (of which the Master is part) and the inner essence or energy. In this realm, the inner essence is most like the Universal Mind or Consciousness. Some call this Consciousness, the Light or God. This Consciousness is the very substance of the universe and gives life and direction to all living things. It is all loving and kind; giving life and vibrancy to the Path. Without this sacred essence all would wither and die. The Spiritual Hierarchy guards this essence and reflects it daily into the world. This is the very fabric of life.

The Path exists to help each student reach completion and ensures the spiritual evolution of the universe. Each traveler must choose to embrace the Light and help others. This action cannot be forced. In part, it is the duty of the Spiritual Hierarchy to ensure that opportunity exists for students to awaken and protect the planet from spiritual harm.

### Right Time, Right Place and Right People

In order for individual spiritual learning to take place, this learning must occur under certain conditions. These conditions include: the right time, right place and right people. This alignment of factors precludes everything else and is contrary to the way things are taught in most other schools. The model of working daily on a subject is useful in some forms of learning, but is limited within the context of spiritual learning and higher knowledge.

In the ordinary classroom, the closest we come to spiritual learning or cognition is the 'Aha!' experience. Ordinarily, this learning experience occurs after a period of readiness and preparation. After the student has been struggling with a problem, suddenly, when the correct combination of factors align, the student grasps what he has been working on-'Aha!' From a spiritual perspective, this experience can be described as a holistic understanding of what is being taught. This coming together occurs on different levels of consciousness simultaneously.

Also, in another way, spiritual learning is unlike other forms of learning. You cannot gain spiritual knowledge simply because you want it and will work hard to get it. While these traits are useful in many things, in this endeavor, this mind-set will only slow you down. You cannot get there with linear thought- it only takes you part of the way. Holistic and spiritual thought have a different set of rules-like those mentioned above.

Higher cognition and intuitive perception develop naturally and gradually over a period of time. With the guidance of a Master, there is a period of preparation and a slow building of impacts; until the student is able to independently perceive on their own.

---

# — B —

# On Mysticism and the Mystery School

Interview with Dr. Stewart Bitkoff @
INSPIRATIONS AND CREATIVE THOUGHTS
with Sadiq M. Alam

[ http://mysticsaint.blogspot.com/2008/10/on-mysticism-and-mystery-school.html ]

"The goal of the mystical school is the completed person. The completed person has added a degree of spiritual development to their other capacities. This spiritual development is accomplished through an interaction between the Master, the student and Path." - *Dr. Stewart Bitkoff, from his article: "The Mystical School."*

The following is excerpts from an interview with Dr. Stewart Bitkoff, author of the book "A Commuter's Guide to Enlightenment". Dr. Bitkoff is a doctoral graduate in education, an expert in Therapeutic Recreation, Psychiatric Rehab and Psychiatric Treatment

For years, Dr. Bitkoff studied in two modern mystical schools and was designated to help make available aspects of this secret, inner teaching. Professionally, Dr. Bitkoff has taught in various colleges and universities and worked to help the mentally ill integrate their altered state of consciousness into the physical world. In this interview we touch upon mysticism, mystical schools, the Sufi path and the training of mystics.

*\*(Portions edited for grammar, contextual clarity, and condensed from 2 parts.)*

SADIQ: *The word 'mystic' to the general public creates a lot of confusion. If you were to define this term, how would you describe who or what is a 'mystic?'*

DR. STEWART BITKOFF: The word mystic comes from the word mystery; someone who seeks the mystery. What is the mystery? For different people, this is always different. In terms of the mystery school, the student or traveler was/is taught about the mystery of the universe- in hidden, mysterious, non-traditional, ways. Throughout history, traditions abound concerning the mystery schools and what was actually taught there. Keep in mind, if this knowledge was not a mystery and others knew about it; for many practitioners often it would mean death. Throughout time, traditionalists would have required the execution of those involved, because what was taught was not the standard form of religion. It was the inner current, or perception, connection, and alignment with the Truth/Light.

My teacher used to say, as he reflected the Light across our hearts, this was the mystery and learning that was taught in the great pyramids.

*When one uses the word 'mystic' in the context of Sufi path - what is the emphasis here?*

People always need to define something; put it into a category so it is understood. Followers of the Path are given names so others will understand what is going on. Sufis do not call themselves Sufis; this is considered egotistical, limiting, and not accurate. Others have called Sufis the original mystics; once again, this is an attempt by them to understand what the Sufi is doing.

For followers of this Path, the mystery or emphasis is connection with the Divine; Love of God and direct perception of the Truth/Light. The traveler does not believe there is a God/Light; the traveler knows there is a God/Light. Through the intervention of the Teacher, the traveler connects, is one with this primordial energy, and aligns their inner essence (heart) with the Light.

As love, in a worldly context matures, the lover does not say, I think/believe that I love my wife and daughter, the traveler knows he/she loves their family member. It is the same with spiritual studies and knowledge of God. We do not talk about God, or say we believe, we know and experience the Divine Essence.

### What does a mystical school consist of?

A mystical school consists of a teacher/Master, student/traveler, and the Path; which is an aspect of the Light. It is the Baraka (grace) of the Path, which the teacher uses to do his/her work. The Light is the life force and the way we connect with God; fused together in a glorious way- which is perceived, known, experienced and loved. Here words are limitations. Just as Christians speak of the Holy Trinity: Father, Son, and Holy Spirit; the Path, Light, and God are One; interconnected and expressed on infinite levels. The traveler speaks of glimpsing only a small fraction of this, a lock of hair from the beloved.

### Can a person be trained to become a mystic? If the goal of a mystical school is to help train mystics, in this present day, please describe how this is possible.

All learning requires training, innate capacity, preparation, and hard work. It is no different with spiritual studies. Each traveler is born with a life plan or destiny; we come here with an agenda of sorts; some of which we choose and some of which is chosen for us. This life plan or agenda presupposes a skill set, or inner sense of what we like and wish to accomplish. Once again, spiritual studies, mystical training, and any other endeavor are linked through pre-existing factors; some of these factors stretch across lifetimes, experience in other realms, and our present requirements. To answer the question, yes, travelers can be trained to be mystics. This is the natural Way to experience God, before there was formal religion. It has always existed. Does every traveler require this training? Right now. In this present experience? That is up to each traveler and God. Remember, each is given what they require. No one's experience is better than another's; it is different, specifically for them, and guided by the Unseen Forces.

*How do you see the concept of 'a completed person?'*

A completed person has added a level of spiritual capacity and aligns their action with the higher potential. In order for this to occur, the traveler must be balanced and reasonably adjusted to ordinary life. Spiritual capacity is in addition to all other capacities and serves as an integrating factor; a foundation from which a complete life may be lived. We were created to participate in the world; helping to make it a better place, by aligning personal action with the highest potential in each moment. Now, how does one do this sort of thing? That is the mystery and is at the heart of the Path and mystery school. It begins by submission and love. Because we love, we are willing to do for another.

*Your training in the Sufi path is quite unique given that it happened in the heart of the West by an eastern teacher who in Sufi terms was a 'hidden teacher,' and timing wise it was in early 70's, which was also a very unique, changing time (equally true from planetary evolutionary perspective). Tell us something about the nature of this initiation with regard to the Path, teacher and training.*

Basically, there was training in 2 schools. The first part was with the Teacher/Master, occurred at work and lasted for approximately 4 years. This occurred in the early 1970's and was in a state funded psychiatric hospital. The teacher was a psychiatrist from Pakistan and his father was a Sufi; 3 years into things we learned he was a Muslim. There were many other students; some of whom accepted what was taught and others left it for something else. There was no emphasis upon a particular religion, exotic clothing, or giving money to fund a specific church/mosque/synagogue. When we were asked to donate something, it was always up to whatever charity we wished and at a comfortable level. We were taught to love God and experience God in every moment; the teacher taught by shining the Light upon our hearts and other experiences; we learned how to perceive our own spiritual nature and connect with God.

One day, the teacher called us into his office and said it was time to move onto the next teacher. We were to write the Society for Sufi Studies and await instructions. After 6 months time, instructions came to read and totally familiarize myself with 20 books written by Idries Shah; a list was included. At first, I balked at this, having read 5 books by Shah and wondered why I needed to do all of this. Anyway, in time I set about this task which took over 10 years. In the process, I learned much from this material: it is a complete body of work, which according to Shah, supersedes all other previous Sufi material. It is a complete course, if you will, of what the western seeker needs to travel the Path. When Shah died in 1996, many people considered him to be the Sufi Teacher of the Age and his job, in part, was to offer this material to the west.

Interestingly enough, I am working on a book entitled, *Sufism: Path of the Spiritual Traveler In Everyday Life*, which speaks to the point of my initiation in the first school, and different experiences and thoughts in both schools; and how this learning has woven its way into my life. The manuscript is awaiting publication.

Our first teacher is still alive and when approached by possible students, tells them to read certain titles by Shah (*The Sufis, Learning How to Learn, The Way of the Sufi, and A Perfumed Scorpion*); he no longer entertains questions from us about the path, and is very gracious and concerned about all of us. He still chooses to remain anonymous.

One of the first things students will say is, look I want spiritual experience, not reading from books. The books answer this question: first you have to 'learn how to learn' or have the right attitude/posture about this sort of thing. It requires a serious or mature student/traveler- who is able to suspend or push aside certain thoughts and prejudices.

*To my understanding, this (the Sufi Path you walked) was a very harmonious, universal, totally non-dogmatic... what one may call 'Organic Spirituality.' Am I correct to characterize it? When you look back at it now, how do you describe it?*

You know, this is the natural path to God/Light; it is the path before there was organized religion; and is the inner current of religious training. Consider if you never heard of Shah, or read this interview, don't you think this experience or way of spiritual knowing, if you required it, would be made available? It is very simple and very complex. "'Love God with all your heart and soul." The first commandment. If the concept/word God is bothersome substitute "The Light."

Look, we all have an innate spiritual nature, and what we are discussing is maximizing our potential in this area; in order that this capacity becomes part of every day life. This learning and capacity is to be used across our lifetime- to help self and others.

*According to your personal experience and from your own walking in the Path - how would you describe to a western lay person if you were asked, 'What is the Sufi Way?'*

My daughter has been interested in the Sufi Way for sometime, and she is always offering examples of trying to explain what she believes/experiences to others, who ask about her beliefs. This is not a simple thing. Basically, we are trying to put into words, what other teachers have called an 'essence' an 'attitude' or 'way of experiencing reality.' Some have said, 'Sufism is learned in the company of other Sufis.'

*Appendix B. On Mysticism and the Mystery School*

To me, Sufism is the experience of ultimate reality through your own innate spirituality. There is a part of us that knows where it came from and where it is going, and when this part is awakened, slowly, it becomes the inner voice that knows the way home. Sufism is using your own inner, spiritual voice to enrich your daily life and the lives of others.

**What is the future of Sufism in the world today, especially in the West?**

The message of Sufism is a hopeful one; that there is a God, who loves his/her children, and has created a way for his/her children to attain unto Him/Her. Also, there is a Plan for humanity, and this Plan involves the awakening of certain capacities within each traveler, one person at a time, to help make this world a better place. Traditionally, the Sufis are the guardians of this Plan and help make sure that it is accomplished.

For the western traveler, Sufism holds the promise of an individual relationship with Ultimate Reality. Always, this relationship is one of Love, Joy, and Forgiveness. There is no boundary here and each traveler is created with an individual potential: to love, work, experience, and serve. Each is a child of Light; the son and daughter of a King who creates their own reality.

This world is a giant market place, and we are free to do whatever we like. Within our free will choice, we create our own reality moment by moment. The problems of the world and life, for the most part, are the creation of individual travelers. Our responsibility is to create reality, that is our mission, and the problems of greed, destruction, war, and hunger for the most part are solvable by travelers, if they chose collectively to do so.

In each moment there is potential, and to choose the higher destiny, is the Sufi Call.

*What do you think would be the correct vision to meet the spiritual thirst of American people in terms of spiritual orientation and training?*

America is a special place; America offers the spiritual freedom, alive in each person's heart to choose what is best for himself and others. Here in this country, each traveler can freely choose their own life and how they wish to live it.

Our higher destiny is alignment with Ultimate Truth and helping others. Some Americans quickly forget that this country was founded by travelers who wanted to be free of the restrictions, rules, and the tyranny of others. Leaving the countries of Europe, with their monarchies and religious authoritarianism, these travelers chose to find a world where they could help create a reality more like the spiritual freedom within.

The message of Sufism is the same; you are a child of the Light; free to create your own reality; and when you help another, in the name of the Light, you rise higher than the angels. The spirit of Sufism transcends individual religion and creed; it is the song of love, freedom and joy that is alive in your heart.

According to some reports and tradition, there was a hidden Sufi presence on the Mayflower and in the writing the Declaration of Independence. So you see America and Sufism have been entwined since the beginning; mysteriously the Plan unfolds, and each rises up, like the smoke from the evening fire, becoming a better version of itself.

### Who is Stewart Bitkoff?

'Who is Stewart Bitkoff?' This question makes me laugh; I have been trying to figure that out for 64 years. When you find him, tell me, so I too might meet him.

To date, the closest I have come to understanding myself is the following: I am a spiritual traveler, who has stopped to rest in the shade, with a few stories to tell, a few people to love and kiss, then, I must be on my way. On the other side, awaiting me is another adventure: with some old friends and some new ones as well.

*Lets consider an average American person (or Westerner if you like) who in his or her being feels very spiritual. Is in the process of discovering their own human, inner nature which is essentially spiritual; yet this person has a lot of wounds around conventional religion, has a negative association with the very word and notion of 'God' as a result of misuse, abuse, mixing falsehood with truth, by the institutional religious organization and society. What and how would you offer advice to this person who is drawn to his or her original spiritual nature, Buddha nature in far Eastern terms or 'Fitrah' (basic natural disposition of spirituality instilled in all human hearts) in Quranic terms?*

First, feeling spiritual is different than being spiritual. Feeling is an emotional state and spiritual experience is different than feelings. Often, emotions must be stilled for a time, so the spiritual essence may step forward.

Second, God/Light is different than religion and the actions of individual travelers; to understand who you are and the spiritual potential within, you must go beyond religion, country, family, expectation and individual desire; these are the sources of your wounds and hurt. Within is your own individual answer and healing to the question about the world's injustice.

Remember, in this journey we are both jailor and redeemer; we have the potential to go beyond both.

Yes, it is true that religion has caused much harm and hurt; but it has also helped many along their journey. I too was injured, but it was precisely this hurt which pushed me to find my inner spiritual nature; was this pain then not useful in my journey?

*What is the concept and goal of enlightenment in the Sufi path or in a mystic school like the ones you were trained in?*

Within our framework, enlightenment comes in small, gradual impacts, flashes of intuitive insight, spiritual states, and knowing.

Simplistically, enlightenment is added spiritual capacity, which is natural, and useful in every day life. According to Idries Shah, 'if enlightenment were to come in a big burst it would be disruptive.'

Within our training, we were taught how to turn every day activities, like driving to work, into spiritual practice. It was a matter of intention and focus; who were we doing these activities for?

Often, travelers think that enlightenment will free them from pains and sorrows of ordinary life, which is not the case. On this Path, spiritual responsibilities are in addition to those of every day life. Life is a multi-level experience and we are to experience it all.

***Looking at the contemporary world as it is, in its physical, emotional, political or cosmic makeup - what troubles you most?***

What troubles me most, in this contemporary world, is that we do not seem to learn from the mistakes of the past. The problems of greed, self-interest, and travelers wishing to take from others, has been with us since the beginning.

History has shown that it is in everyone's best interest, that our neighbor is fed, has medical services, and has the opportunity for education, work and a full life. If this is not so, then eventually, these people will rise up guided by an opportunist leader to take what has been withheld. Then, the cycle of injustice will start up again.

The problems of the world are solved only by making better people; this is done one person at a time. Remember, if someone is hungry or sick, first you must help with their primary need, then, move onto other things like work, education, and proper shelter and, finally you achieve a spirituality that transcends personal interest.

If you want to help make the world better, first work on yourself. Use each moment to reach higher and help your neighbor. It's pretty simple. You know, the Golden Rule. Help yourself and help your neighbor. Leave your camp site a little cleaner than when you found it. Give rather than take.

A better world starts with each of us; taking better care of our self, first, then helping others, second. Why haven't we learned this yet? That is the Sufi message: treat others as equal to our self.

### Who is your most favorite personality and why?

My favorite personality or personalities are those travelers who emanate love. I have been most affected by those individuals who freely give to others, first, out of boundless love. Often it was a simple act, making a sandwich because I was hungry or inquiring about my day and life. My mother was like this; so are my wife; my spiritual teacher; and countless others who I have been fortunate enough to meet. These are the people who have affected me, offering a hand when I have fallen, and sharing my life in countless ways.

*Imagine one of your earlier spiritual guides has left his body some significant amount of time back. Since then you have walked quite a lot and gathered all ranges of human experiences, as we all do as long as we inhabit this body. If you were to meet your spiritual teacher again, today in a peaceful park what question (or questions) would your heart ask him?*

If I was to meet my spiritual teacher, in a peaceful park, and we were to share a quiet moment together on a bench, it would not be to ask a question.

Slowly, a tear would fall from my eye, and I would thankfully whisper: "Now, I understand."

———————————

Parts 1 & 2 reprinted together with permission of Sadiq M. Alam, Mystic Saint Blogspot, http://mysticsaint.blogspot.com.

# — C —
# Notes

## Introduction

Stewart Bitkoff, *A Commuter's Guide to Enlightenment*, Llewellyn: Worldwide, 2008.

This Sufi Proverb appears online at *Sufi Spiritual Quotes*, www.katinkahesselink.net/sufi/quotes.html, accessed 10/3/08.

## Chapter 1: My Religious Training

None

## Chapter 2: Getting Started

"The Sufi Quest" by Mevlevi Ustad Hilmi, taken from Idries Shah, *Thinkers of the East*, New York: Penguin and cited in Robert Cecil, Richard Rieu and David Wade, *The King's Son*, London: Octagon Press, 1981, p. 7.

Aldous Huxley, *The Perennial Philosophy*, New York: Harper & Brothers Publishers, 1945.

Mulla Nasruddin Story #152 appears online at *200 Jokes of Mulla Nasruddin*, www.otoons.com/joke&game/mulla_nasruddin.htm, accessed 8/31/09.


## Chapter 3: Our First Conversation- Life is all About Me!

Neale Donald Walsch, *The Complete Conversations With God*, Charlottesville, VA: Hampton Roads Publishing, 2005.

Idries Shah quote appears online at *Sufi Spiritual Quotes*, www.katinkakesselink.net/sufi/quotes.html, accessed 8/31/09.

Robert E. Ornstein and David Sobel, *Healthy Pleasures*, Reading, Massachusetts: Perseus Books, 1989.


## Chapter 4: Our Conversation Continues- Hunger Pains that Can't Be Cured With Food.

Traditional saying taken from James Fadiman and Robert Frager, *Essential Sufism*, San Francisco: HarperSanFrancisco, 1997, p. 98.


## Chapter 5: Sufism and the Mystical School Begin to Ease the Hunger

Abdul-Wahab T. Tiryaqi quote taken from Idries Shah, *Sufi Thought and Action*, London: Octagon Press, 1990, p. 213.

Sirdar Ikbal Ali Shah quote taken from Shah, *Sufi Thought and Action*, p.178.

## Chapter 6: Sufis are Everyday People Living Life as a Prayer

Quote taken from Farid Ud-Din Attar, *The Conference of the Birds.* New York: Samuel Weiser, Inc., 1969, p. 103

Idries Shah, *The Sufis*, London: The Octagon Press, 1977.

Hoda Azizian quote taken from Shah, *Sufi Thought and Action*, p. 125.

## Chapter 7: Discovering and Choosing Our Higher Selves in an Expectation & Rewards Kind of World

Quote taken from Attar, *The Conference of the Birds*, p. 45

Al-Ghazzali quote taken from James Fadiman and Robert Frager, *Essential Sufism*, p. 59.

Muhammad quote appears in Fadiman and Frager, *Essential Sufism*, p. 89.

## Chapter 8: Are You Really Saying We Can Co-Create Our Reality?

Idries Shah, *Knowing How to Know*, London: The Octagon Press, 1998, p. 92.

## Chapter 9: Ancient Teachings Need a 21st Century Update

Sheik Ismail Hakki quote taken from Idries Shah, *The Way of the Sufi*, Penguin Arkana: Paperback and cited in Cecil, Rieu, and Wade, *The King's Son*, p.16.

Jiddu Krishnamurti interview with *JK: BBC Transcript*, cited in Cecil, Rieu, and Wade, *The King's Son*, p. 104.

For a complete discussion of the concept, 'learning how to learn,' see Idries Shah, *Learning How to Learn*, London: Octagon Press, 1978.

Two stories about finding a guru/teacher, found in Idries Shah, *Knowing How to Know*, p.21, and p. 228.

## Chapter 10: Submission of Will, Freedom of Choice and Real Life Spiritual Experience

Dag Hammarskjold quote taken from *Markings*, cited in Cecil, Rieu, and Wade, *The King's Son*, p.107.

Robert E. Ornstein, *Multimind*, Boston: Houghton Miflin, 1986.

Dhu-l-Nun quote taken from Fadiman and Frager, *Essential Sufism*. p. 36

Jami quote taken from Fadiman and Frager, *Essential Sufism*, p. 39.

Hujwiri quote taken from Fadiman and Frager, *Essential Sufism*, p. 36.

## Chapter 11: Ordinary People Shining Extraordinary Light into the World

Khayyam quote taken from Shah, *Knowing How to Know*, p. 219.

Shabistari quote taken from Shah, *Knowing How to Know*, p. 219.

Attar quote appears in Fadiman and Frager, *Essential Sufism*, p. 247.

## Chapter 12: Proof, Miracles, Belief and Moving On From First School

Chawan Thurlnas quote taken from Shah, *Sufi Thought and Action*, p. 96.

Al-Ghazzali quote appears in Shah, *Knowing How to Know*, p.319.

## Chapter 13: Everyday Spirituality

Rumi quote taken from Fadiman and Frager, *Essential Sufism*, p. 244.

Reference to St. John of the Cross Poem: 'The Living Flame of Love,' appearing in Kiernan Kavanaugh and Otilio Rodriguez, *The Collected Works of St. John of the Cross*, Washington, DC: ICS Publications, 1973, p. 573.

## Chapter 14: Traveler's Creed

Kabir quote from Fadiman and Frager, *Essential Sufism*, p. 213.

Modern traditional saying from Fadiman and Frager, *Essential Sufism*, p. 48.

Al-Hujwiri quote taken from Shah, *Knowing How to Know*, p. 220.

## Story: The Star Child

Gandhi quote accessed 1/21/10 online:
www.allgreatquotes.com/mahatma_gandhi_quotes3.html

Made in the USA
Lexington, KY
29 July 2013